CHURCH IN ORDINARY TIME

CHURCH IN ORDINARY TIME

A Wisdom Ecclesiology

Amy Plantinga Pauw

WILLIAM B. EERDMANS PUBLISHING COMPANY
GRAND RAPIDS, MICHIGAN

Wm. B. Eerdmans Publishing Co.
2140 Oak Industrial Drive NE, Grand Rapids, Michigan 49505
www.eerdmans.com

26 25 24 23 22 21 20 19 18 17   1 2 3 4 5 6 7 8 9 10

ISBN 978-0-8028-7186-2

Library of Congress Cataloging-in-Publication Data

Names: Pauw, Amy Plantinga, author.
Title: Church in ordinary time : a wisdom ecclesiology / Amy Plantinga Pauw.
Description: Grand Rapids : Eerdmans Publishing Co., 2017. |
    Includes bibliographical references and index.
Identifiers: LCCN 2017020666 | ISBN 9780802871862 (pbk. : alk. paper)
Subjects: LCSH: Church. | Christian life.
Classification: LCC BV600.3 .P38 2017 | DDC 262—dc23
    LC record available at https://lccn.loc.gov/2017020666

For Alan, churchgoing realist

Contents

CONTENTS

Acknowledgments

B ooks are never solo efforts. I am grateful to the Henry Luce Foundation for a fellowship that gave me time to write this book, and for providing helpful opportunities to discuss my project during its early stages. I also thank Louisville Presbyterian Seminary for granting me sabbatical leave. I first presented some of the material in this book as the T. F. Torrance Lectures at the University of Aberdeen, Scotland, the Grider Winget Lectures at Nazarene Theological Seminary in Kansas City, Missouri, and the Kerr Lectures at the University of Glasgow, Scotland. I am grateful for those invitations and for the opportunities for dialogue that they opened up.

Melisa Scarlott and Timothy McNinch helped me prepare the manuscript. As I wrote this book, I was surrounded by many wise people: Brad Wigger, Carol Cook, Chris Elwood, Christine Hong, Cláudio Carvalhaes, Cliff Kirkpatrick, Kathryn Johnson, Marty Soards, Shannon Craigo-Snell, Ted Smith, Timothy McNinch, and Willie Jennings, each of whom read some or all of the manuscript and helped make it better. I am in their debt. I offer a special word of appreciation to Ted Smith, who has been an invaluable source of counsel and encouragement since the inception of this project. I thank James Ernest at Eerdmans for his generous editorial assistance.

My pastor, Jane Larsen-Wigger, has shown me over many years what it looks like to hold the theological and the concrete together in church life. I hope this book reflects some of what I have learned from her. Alan, Clara, Andrea, and Emily have been my beloved companions along the way, providing the humor and solace I needed to keep going.

AMY PLANTINGA PAUW

Why Ordinary Time Matters

> *To know*
> *That which before us lies in daily life*
> *Is the prime wisdom.*
>
> —JOHN MILTON, *Paradise Lost*

Communities of Christian faith that follow the liturgical calendar spend most of their life in "ordinary time." About one-third of the liturgical year, stretching from Advent to Epiphany and then again from Ash Wednesday to Pentecost, encompasses the feasts that commemorate the great drama of the reconciliation and promised consummation of the world in Christ. The remaining two-thirds—a shorter period from Epiphany to Ash Wednesday, and a longer stretch from Pentecost to the beginning of Advent, thirty-three or thirty-four weeks in total—is designated "ordinary time." In contemporary usage, "ordinary" means usual, not special; but in this phrase it has the sense of numbered, counted out (think of "ordinal" numbers). Ordinary time has been regarded as a mere placeholder, a way to mark time between the theologically important parts of the church year. In this book I give ordinary time theological significance in its own right by connecting it to the doctrine of creation. Ordinary time serves as a metaphor for our creaturely existence as it is sustained by God's creative blessing and calling. An ordinary-time ecclesiology emphasizes that the church lives in the gap between the resurrection of Jesus and the last things as God's creature. I trace the significance of this creaturely dimension of the church's life in different ways through the whole book. When, in part 3 of the book, my focus shifts back to the rhythms of the entire liturgical year, I likewise expand and enrich its meaning by way of this theological emphasis on creaturehood.

At the center of any ecclesiology, the word "church" poses a terminological problem for which there is no easy resolution. My goal is to talk about "church" in a way that is both theological and concrete. Some write easily about "the church" or "the Church" (capitalized), implying that it (or "she") is a singular, sharply defined entity. Looking around us, though, we see many local congregations, regional associations, national denominations, and global communions, not all so sharply bounded and defined. In this book, therefore, I will be using the term "church"—lowercase and usually without any article—to denote the publicly visible, though not sharply definable, reality of self-identified communities of Christian faith spread across time and space. As Donald MacKinnon has insisted, ecclesiology should focus on actual people, those "sustained and illuminated, irritated and sometimes infuriated by particular traditions of Christian life and thought."[1] Theologically, *church* refers to communities gathered and sustained by God, communities who practice their faith by the power of the Holy Spirit in response to God's grace in Jesus Christ. As this book will emphasize, creaturehood is basic to church's theological identity. Ecclesial practice and mission are responses made possible by an ongoing creaturely dependence on God. At the same time, *church* is an appropriate subject of historical and cultural analysis, patient of approaches that are used in examining other forms of human community. To affirm the theological identity of church is not to retreat to a timeless spiritual realm in which questions about the daily, practical dimensions of human associations do not apply. A theological emphasis on creaturehood helps hold together the theological and concrete dimensions of church.

Formal ecclesiologies have largely neglected this ordinary-time dimension of Christian life—to their detriment. In so doing, they ignore the primordial and ongoing graciousness of God's work as Creator. John Webster has noted that "a doctrine of the church is only as good as the doctrine of

---

1. D. M. MacKinnon, *The Stripping of the Altars* (London: Collins, Fontana Library, 1969), 66.

God which underlies it." He warns against settling for "a selection of those divine attributes or acts which coordinate with a certain ecclesiological proposal."[2] By eclipsing God's creative mode of relating, ecclesiology generally operates with a truncated doctrine of God, and this truncation has unfortunate theological consequences. An account of church in ordinary time encourages Christians to acknowledge and reflect on the fullness of their relationship to the triune God, which includes their relationship to God as Creator. It prompts an acknowledgment of commonality with other creatures of God. It encourages Christians to think about the texture of their daily life in community, and about how spiritual transformation characteristically happens by God's presence in the ordinary processes of the world. From the perspective of ordinary time, there is no disconnection between the reality of God's active presence, on the one hand, and the need for human discernment, struggle, and patience, on the other. An account of church in ordinary time is ecclesiology for days when, in Ellen Davis's words, "water does not pour forth from rocks and angels do not come for lunch."[3] Most days in church life are like that.

An ordinary-time ecclesiology readily claims its own creaturely situatedness. There is no fulcrum outside the flow of nature and history from which an account of church can be theorized. Christian communities of faith are culturally shaped incubators of theological knowledge. The theological pedagogy that occurs in them is intrinsically tied to social processes; it happens both deliberately and unintentionally. It is about cultural and bodily formation of desires at least as much as clarification of beliefs. Nowhere in the teachings of Christian theology is this communal shaping more evident than in reflection on church. Ecclesiology is a part of Christian dogmatics where oral tradition and bodily habituation most directly mold formal theological instincts and conclusions, whether this molding is acknowledged or not. Ecclesiology is theology at its most inductive.

2. John Webster, "The Church and the Perfection of God," in *The Community of the Word: Toward an Evangelical Ecclesiology*, ed. Mark Husbands and Daniel J. Treier (Grand Rapids: Baker Academic, 2005), 78. I do not claim that Webster is in full agreement with my ecclesiological appropriation of his counsel.

3. Ellen F. Davis, *Proverbs, Ecclesiastes, and the Song of Songs*, Westminster Bible Companion (Louisville: Westminster John Knox, 2000), 12.

The Point of View of This Book

Since daily life in Christian communities of faith is the context for constructing a theology of church, there is an inevitable circularity to ecclesiological reflection. It always begins in the middle of things, in the flow of communal life and language. My ecclesiological instincts are rooted in my experiences as a well-educated, white, middle-class North American woman in a variety of Reformed Protestant settings. No doubt my years as deacon, Sunday school teacher, and church musician have left their mark on my ecclesiology. My Reformed sensibilities include a heightened awareness of idolatry: God is God, and everything else is not. The presence of God in the created world is never separated from God's activity, and thus is never subject to human control and manipulation. In my theological reflections, I habitually think with the Bible and lean on classic Trinitarian teachings. I trust that God's redemptive purposes extend to oppressive social structures and to the groaning of nonhuman creation. For better *and* for worse, my gender, race, class, liturgical practice, and confessional orientation all help shape what church has been for me over the course of my life, and hence where my ecclesiological reflections begin. Because all ecclesiology begins at home, I will make my larger argument about the theological validity of an ordinary-time ecclesiology with special attention to the distinctive emphases of Reformed theological traditions.

No single person is in a position to write a truly adequate ecclesiology. Even as I claim my Reformed heritage, I recognize my debts to diverse fellow travelers who have greatly challenged and broadened my understanding of church. I am in their debt, and I suspect that it is possible to arrive at many of my ecclesiological conclusions by alternate cultural and confessional routes. Church is a complex, interdependent organism: no part of Christ's body may say to another part, "I have no need of you" (1 Cor. 12:21). Perhaps even more than other Christian teachings, ecclesiology is intrinsically incomplete and resistant to systematization. I offer my articulation of church in ordinary time in an experimental register for the benefit of the greater community of Christ's disciples: "Try looking at church this way."[4] Other Christians will

4. David H. Kelsey takes a similar approach in his theological anthropology; see *Eccentric Existence: A Theological Anthropology*, 2 vols. (Louisville: Westminster John Knox, 2009), 9.

have their own resources and arguments to contribute to this project. The "we" and "us" of this book are aimed at the wider Christian community, and it is this larger cloud of witnesses who will help discern the wisdom or folly of my approach.

As a Reformed Christian, I have inherited a self-relativizing view of church, one that acknowledges the social and cultural relativism of all ecclesial patterns and structures, and approaches them with a rather functional pragmatism. Communities of Christian faith live by tradition and memory, but also by improvisation: church is a community of communities that knows no final form, no fixed patterns of ministry. As Eberhard Busch has pointed out, at the center of being Reformed is a paradoxical openness to relativizing one's own confessional identity: to be strong in one's Reformed identity is to affirm one's ecclesial weakness and incompleteness.[5] According to this view, all expressions of church suffer from creaturely limitations, so that no single strand of the Christian tradition can claim historical or theological completeness. Reformed communities of faith consider themselves partial but genuine expressions of a larger Christian whole. My ecclesiology does not claim completeness—but is offered in service to a larger ecumenical vision.

Ambiguity, including moral ambiguity, is unavoidable in church life. My little corner of church has become increasingly aware of how it has benefited from and abused racial privilege, as well as social and political capital. Now faced with declining membership and theological infighting, it wrestles with the shape of faithful Christian witness in an ecologically threatened and religiously pluralistic world. There are no ecclesial shortcuts in negotiating these earthly challenges, no transcending to an otherworldly plane where they do not matter anymore. An account of church in ordinary time thus resists what Karl Barth calls "ecclesiastical docetism."[6] Docetic ecclesiology shies away from affirming the fully human character of church, on the supposition that the grace of God's presence somehow lifts earthly Christian communities beyond the limitations and struggles of ordinary creaturely life. Too many

---

5. Eberhard Busch, "Reformed Strength in Its Denominational Weakness," in *Reformed Theology: Identity and Ecumenicity*, ed. Wallace Alston and Michael Welker (Grand Rapids: Eerdmans, 2003), 20–33.

6. Karl Barth, *Church Dogmatics*, IV/1 (Edinburgh: T&T Clark, 1956), 653.

ecclesiologies provide accounts of church that seem to have no earthly home. Instead, an ordinary-time ecclesiology adopts an unsentimental realism that acknowledges human infirmity and weakness while remaining grateful for God's gift of creaturely life in community.

Church's Infirmity

The infirmity confessed in an ordinary-time ecclesiology is not confined to creaturely finitude. It also extends to church's peccability, its proneness to sin. A forthright account of its history calls church to repentance. While it is important to theologically distinguish between finitude and sin, both are fully intertwined in earthly ecclesial experience. Finitude is intrinsic to creaturely life: even fully redeemed and glorified creatures remain finite, though they are no longer vulnerable to the suffering endemic to earthly creaturehood. Finitude is not, in itself, a condition from which Christians need to be saved, even as they rightly cry out for deliverance from their earthly suffering. By contrast, sin is an intruder that corrupts and feeds off God's gift of creaturely existence, embedding itself into social structures and personal habits. The earthly narrative of church has no Eden. It begins "after the Fall," and continues through periods of great religious and political turmoil. The earthly church suffers both because of its finitude and because of its sin. An ordinary-time ecclesiology acknowledges the reality of ecclesial sin and attempts to let church scandals and failures, the tragedies and victims of its communal life, enter into ecclesiological reflection. Church's use of its most sacred symbols and traditions is subject to God's judgment. Dogmatic approaches to church need to be intertwined with honest social and pastoral analysis, so that they do not become merely a theological abstraction, or an exercise in justifying and defending specific ecclesial structures and patterns.

Commenting on the Apostles' Creed, John Calvin notes that Christian trust rests finally in God, and therefore Christians do not properly believe *in* the church: "We testify that we believe *in* God because our mind reposes in him as truthful, and our trust rests in him." Church is properly an article of belief only "because often no other distinction can be made between God's children and the ungodly, between his own flock and wild beasts."[7] Hans Küng also underscores the distinction between church and God. Church is God's creature; therefore, it is "not omniscient and omnipotent, not self-sufficient and autonomous, not eternal and sinless. It is not the source of grace and truth, it is not Lord, redeemer and judge, and there can be no question of idolizing it."[8] On earth, church is often hidden under the form of its opposite. God has entrusted Christian communities with the power of the keys (Matt. 16:19), but they can so abuse this trust that in them, according to Calvin, "Christ lies hidden, half buried, the gospel overthrown, piety scattered, the worship of God nearly wiped out."[9] An ordinary-time ecclesiology rejects the theological sleight of hand that says God's church does not sin in itself but only in its members, or that when it sins, it ceases to be God's church. Instead, it affirms that church lives by confession of its sins and assurance of God's pardoning grace—an ecclesiological *simul justus et peccator*. This is not a fatalistic resignation to sinfulness; instead, it is a penitent acknowledgment of the continuing rhythm of confession and forgiveness in church life. Even more fundamentally, an ordinary-time ecclesiology affirms that church lives by the continuing creative grace of God, who sends rain on the just and unjust alike (Matt. 5:45). Even in its sinfulness, church remains God's beloved creature.

Reformed understandings of church have deep debts to Augustine, and have pushed his multivalent ecclesiology in different directions. According to Augustine, we are what we love. In *The City of God*, Augustine contrasts the earthly city, ruled by a competitive, dominating love of self, with the City of God, a community of peace and harmony rooted in the love of God.[10] The eternal City of God casts a shadow on earth, "a prophetic representation of something to come rather than a real presentation in time."[11] This means that

7. John Calvin, *Institutes of the Christian Religion* 4.1.2, ed. John T. McNeill, trans. Ford Lewis Battles (Philadelphia: Westminster Press, 1960), p. 1013.

8. Hans Küng, *The Church*, trans. Ray Ockenden and Rosaleen Ockenden (London: Burns and Oates, 1967), 32–33.

9. Calvin, *Institutes* 4.2.12, p. 1053.

10. This contrast is spelled out succinctly in Augustine, *City of God* 14.28, trans. Gerald G. Walsh, SJ, et al., introduction by Etienne Gilson (Garden City, NY: Image Books, 1958), pp. 321–22.

11. Augustine, *City of God* 15.2, p. 325.

Christ's church on earth is still a pilgrim in the earthly city, its life marked by longing, frustration, and incompleteness. Yet, because of Christ's incarnation, this does not translate into a pious isolation from earthly life. An ordinary-time ecclesiology with Reformed roots follows what might be called a pastoral interpretation of Augustine that recognizes and affirms the earthly church's location in time and in the body.[12] Church in all its untidy visibility is where the triune God is at work. Christians are united to an incarnate Savior by earthly means of grace. To find and follow Christ on earth is to embrace human weakness, just as Christ did. Our desire for God is kindled by the humility and penitence that acknowledge our limitation and sin and orient us toward growth in love by the power of God's grace. Church is the site of this growth through mutual loving service, a persistent willingness to bear each other's sins and burdens. A commitment to pursue creaturely flourishing in the earthly city is combined with confidence in the eschatological promises of God to give us more than we can imagine. An ordinary-time ecclesiology shares this Augustinian commitment to the earthly pilgrim church.

Invisible Church?

John Calvin made his theological commitments to the visible church clear enough.[13] However, other Reformed understandings of church have sometimes claimed Augustine in order to flee the ambiguities of the earthly pilgrim church and take theological refuge in an invisible church composed wholly of God's sanctified elect.[14] God's true church is without spot or wrinkle, cleansed from its earthly weakness and impurities (Eph. 5:27). In Augustinian terms, this true church is the perfected heavenly church of the City of God, its membership visible to God alone. On this model, whatever in the earthly church's life is not defined by the promised perfection of the City of God is not really church.

Reformed theological appeals to the invisible church have sometimes pro-

---

12. I am indebted to Rowan Williams's reading of Augustine. See esp. Williams, "Augustine and the Psalms," *Interpretation* 58, no. 1 (January 2004): 17–27.

13. Calvin, *Institutes* 4.1.2, p. 1013; 4.1.4, p. 1016.

14. See, e.g., the discussion of the ecclesiologies of Herman Hoeksema and Cornelius Van Til in chap. 3.

vided cover for a hypocritical indifference to a lack of reconciliation and visible unity among Christians. The Confession of Belhar (1986), written in the context of South African apartheid, rejects specious Christian appeals to a "spiritual unity" that leaves Christians of different races "alienated from one another for the sake of diversity and in despair of reconciliation."[15] Nineteenth-century American Presbyterian promulgators of the "spirituality of the church" likewise attempted to abstract ecclesial identity from the horrific realities of chattel slavery. The harsh realities of human divisions of nation, class, and race are a scandal for the church of Jesus Christ and are not solved by recourse to an abstract invisible unity, as if issues of injustice, bigotry, and exclusion were peripheral to church's "real" identity. The wider ecclesial unity toward which the notion of the invisible church gestures is upheld by determined efforts on the ground to overcome visible human divisions.

Despite these ecclesiological pitfalls, it is possible for the notion of the invisible church to reinforce, rather than undermine, a primary theological emphasis on the finite, peccable, visible church. As Augustine intended, the invisible church can function as a vital safeguard against Christian perfectionism and sectarianism, reminding Christians that they are not salvation's gatekeepers. In this way the notion of the invisible church can serve both as a corrective to parochial and exclusionary church practices that attempt to limit the scope of divine grace, and as a comfort to those who have been victims of this exclusion. God's gracious intentions for church always exceed what its life instantiates.

Within a pastoral interpretation of Augustine's ecclesiology, the notion of the invisible church functions to head off the violence and hypocrisy of premature human attempts to identify the precise boundaries of church by winnowing out the wheat from the tares (Matt. 13:24–30). Here, the concept of the invisible church is useful primarily as an acknowledgment of the finitude and weakness endemic to creaturehood. Christian communities of faith endure periods of both outward persecution and inward corruption that so veil or deform their appearance that church can be difficult to see. Calvin asks: "How long after Christ's coming was it hidden without form? How often has it since that time been so oppressed by wars, seditions, and heresies that it did not shine forth at all?" "The church cannot always be pointed to with

---

15. The Presbyterian Church (USA), *New Book of Confessions*, 10.4, p. 302.

the finger."[16] Conversely, when a particular Christian community attains great political and moral influence, the notion of the invisible church can also be useful in resisting the pretentions of any ecclesial instantiation to finality. Acknowledging the provisional nature of its life in the earthly city is an ongoing part of church's faithfulness.

Wendell Berry vividly captures an ordinary-time understanding of the invisible church in his novel *Jayber Crow*. The title character is sitting in the sanctuary where he has worshiped for most of his life and has a vision of "all the people gathered there who had ever been there . . . in all the times past and to come, all somehow there in their own time and in all time and in no time."[17] The doctrine of invisibility in this sense serves to remind Christians that church is a community they have neither created nor chosen, a reality that is always far *bigger* than what Christians in any particular context are able to see or acknowledge.

Because God's ultimate aim is not the absorption of all creaturely existence into church, even the broadest notion of the invisible church cannot claim to encompass the full flow of God's grace toward creation. An ordinary-time interpretation of Augustine situates his ecclesiology within his broader celebration of the beauty and goodness of creation. Even the lowly gnat and flea can proclaim, "God made me!"[18] Creaturely beauty and goodness, and even creaturely existence itself, are dim reflections of the perfect being and beauty and goodness of God.[19] Nothing that exists is wholly bereft of the perfections of its Creator, even amidst the conflict and misery of the earthly city. In this life, the two cities are entangled with each other. Christians are not to disdain the earthly city, but to recognize that, "as mortal life is the same for all, there ought to be common cause between the two cities in what concerns our purely human living."[20] The peace of the earthly city is partial and provisional, but still a good worth seeking and rejoicing in—both for Christians and for their earthly neighbors.

16. Calvin, *Institutes*, "Prefatory Address to King Francis I of France," 25.

17. Wendell Berry, *Jayber Crow: A Novel* (Washington, DC: Counterpoint, 2000), 164.

18. Augustine, "Commentary on Psalm 148," *Nicene and Post-Nicene Fathers*, First Series, vol. 8 (repr. ed., Peabody, MA: Hendrickson Publishers, 1994), 676.

19. Augustine, *Confessions* 11.6, trans. Maria Boulding (Hyde Park, NY: New City Press, 2001), p. 288.

20. Augustine, *City of God* 19.17, p. 464.

Wisdom Books and Wisdom Ecclesiology

Christians have developed ways of reading the Bible that undermine serious theological attention to our identity as God's creatures, and this poses a problem for an ordinary-time ecclesiology. Though this problem is not confined to modern Western theology, the Western preoccupation with the category of history, and in particular with the history of salvation (*Heilsgeschichte*), provides an acute example of this neglect of creaturehood. Within a Western sin-salvation framework, historical communication is God's paradigmatic means of relating to creatures, and human redemption is God's paradigmatic act. This preoccupation with God's words and deeds in human history has flattened biblical interpretation and truncated theological understanding of the scope of God's dealings with creaturely reality, often referred to as "God's economy."

An ordinary-time ecclesiology enlarges the patterns governing the reading of Scripture beyond the category of salvation history. As George Tinker points out, this means that space, as well as time, has to become a primary theological category.[21] God's special purposes for Israel and church are always penultimate to God's larger purposes for the life and well-being of all peoples. On an even broader scale, God's economy of communication with humanity falls within the larger economy of God's work of creating, sustaining, and embracing the entire cosmic order. Church needs to takes its place within this larger economy, and this involves broadening its identity as God's covenant community. Made heirs of the covenant sealed in Jesus Christ, church also affirms the ongoing validity of the Noachic covenant, "the everlasting covenant between God and every living creature of all flesh that is on the earth" (Gen. 9:16). Church is an heir to this wider covenant as well, and the implications of this dimension of its covenantal identity deserve theological attention.

The hermeneutical emphasis on the history of human salvation has encouraged a neglect of certain canonical books. In particular, the Wisdom books Job, Proverbs, and Ecclesiastes were until rather recently viewed as stepchildren of the canon, awkward presences whose concerns were largely

---

21. George E. Tinker, *Spirit and Resistance: Political Theology and American Indian Liberation* (Minneapolis: Fortress, 2004), esp. 93–99.

alien to the center of Israel's faith. As John Bright put it in the 1960s, "some parts of the Old Testament are far less clearly expressive of Israel's distinctive understanding of reality than others, some parts (and one thinks of such a book as Proverbs) seem to be only peripherally related to it, while others (for example, Ecclesiastes) even question its essential features."[22] Bright's discomfort with these biblical books is understandable, given his interpretive framework. Missing from the biblical Wisdom books are key elements in Israel's salvation history that have in turn supplied the crucial link to New Testament portrayals of Jesus and church: the covenant with Abraham, the Exodus from Egypt, the giving of the law, the stories of the kings of Israel, the exile and return, and prophetic promises for future blessing. Also missing in canonical Wisdom is attention to cultic purity and correct worship: the focus of faith's expression is not the worshiping assembly, but the ordinary daily settings of home, field, and marketplace. Given the usual assumptions and moves of Christian reflection about church, it is difficult to think of a part of Scripture with less ecclesiological promise.

Yet the distinctive profile of canonical Wisdom is precisely why these books serve as a biblical anchor for an ordinary-time ecclesiology. An ordinary-time ecclesiology is a wisdom ecclesiology, and I will use these terms interchangeably. The horizon of Job, Proverbs, and Ecclesiastes is creation.[23] In these books, the main emphasis is not on "originating creation,"[24] but on God's ongoing work of creation, in which God continues to relate to and sustain all that God has made. Attention to these books helps keep the cosmic scope of God's economy and the creaturely asymmetry of church's relationship to God in view. These books do not speak with one voice. Though

---

22. John Bright, *The Authority of the Old Testament* (Nashville: Abingdon, 1967), 136. I explore these themes further in *Proverbs and Ecclesiastes*, Belief: A Theological Commentary on the Bible (Louisville: Westminster John Knox, 2015).

23. I will also be drawing on the deuterocanonical Wisdom books Sirach and Wisdom of Solomon, though their theological profile is different. In Sirach the figure of Wisdom is identified with Torah, and finds her resting place in Israel. Wisdom of Solomon retells Israel's salvation history as the story of Wisdom's redeeming acts. Both books recognize Israel's traditions of prophecy and prayer.

24. Terence Fretheim, *God and World in the Old Testament: A Relational Theology of Creation* (Nashville: Abingdon, 2005), 5. Fretheim distinguishes three modes of God's creative work: originating, continuing, and completing.

they all stay within the framework of a theology of creation, their differences illustrate the plasticity of this framework. In their different ways, these books concern themselves with daily human life in all its creaturely interconnections. This includes relationships within human communities, but also relationships with nonhuman creation. They wrestle with the ambiguities of created, temporal, and limited existence. God's call to creatures, echoed in these biblical books, is to cultivate the wisdom that is conducive to their own flourishing and the flourishing of all creation. These canonical biblical texts, along with Sirach and Wisdom of Solomon, orient an ordinary-time ecclesiology. Even when they are not appealed to explicitly, they hum along in the background, helping to guard against idealized, triumphalist, and abstract accounts of church.

Church shares in the call to cultivate wisdom for daily life. Church exists in the quotidian, defined by David Kelsey as "a society of fellow creatures that have parity with one another in being valued by God and parity in being radically contingent on God's ongoing creativity for their sheer existence."[25] By anchoring itself in biblical wisdom, an ordinary-time ecclesiology resists the ecclesiological temptation to center its attention on what makes Christians different from other creatures, or even on what makes them less creaturely! It also resists defining church's raison d'être in terms of a scriptural grand narrative of salvation history. "Sin, and therefore church" is not an adequate logic for ecclesiology. The most fundamental presupposition for ecclesial existence is God's ongoing creativity. A wisdom ecclesiology calls church to embrace its radical contingency and its parity with other creatures, and to respond to God's wise agency as Creator with trust and praise, pursuing creaturely wisdom in its own life.

The pursuit of this wisdom propels church beyond itself into the world. The Wisdom literature testifies that God's creative concern and engagement do not stop at the cultural and ethnic boundaries of Israel. Nor does the human search for wisdom. Carole Fontaine finds in Israel's wisdom traditions an "intellectual ecumenism," a willingness to share intellectual resources across boundaries of culture and religion. Egypt and Mesopota-

---

25. Kelsey, *Eccentric Existence*, 213. My wisdom ecclesiology is indebted to Kelsey's theological analysis of canonical Wisdom literature as a framework for understanding God's creative relationship with humanity.

mia were the motherlands of wisdom in the ancient Near East, and there is general agreement that Israel's Wisdom literature is internationally inspired. Fontaine notes that the sages of Israel "were wise precisely because they honed their thought on the words of the sages and the experience of the cultures that preceded and surrounded them."[26] In the "Words to the Wise" section of Proverbs, for example, scholars have discovered direct literary dependence on the Egyptian wisdom text known as *Instruction of Amenemope*, written late in the second millennium BCE.[27] Israel's piety was capacious enough to include theological reflection that was not tied to Israel's self-understanding as a special covenant people of God. Instead of calling Israel to separate itself from and reject the ways of its neighbors, the Wisdom books model a critical acceptance of the insights and teachings of other nations. What God intends Israel to learn about creaturely life binds them to people from other cultures and religious traditions, making Israel their debtor in its search for wisdom. The biblical Wisdom books also encourage Christian communities of faith to embrace an intellectual ecumenism, to learn from and work side by side with other communities for the sake of creaturely flourishing.

Like an ordinary-time ecclesiology, the creation theology of Job, Proverbs, and Ecclesiastes begins in the middle of things. It does not speculate about the origins of the everyday world, nor does it postulate a "paradise lost" in which human existence was without suffering or sin. Nor does it assume that human creatures are on a trajectory to actualize their true identity in some future context. Instead, the Wisdom books affirm God's creative power and presence in ordinary daily life. They do not denigrate this creaturely life, but they are realistic about its limitations and moral ambiguity. In the face of the suffering and injustice of creaturely life, lament and protest are called for. Job cries out his bewilderment and grief over his unjust suffering, and Qohelet, the narrator of Ecclesiastes, protests "the grievous ills" of oppression and poverty. A wisdom ecclesiology likewise insists on the place of lament and protest in church life.

26. Carole R. Fontaine, *Smooth Words: Women, Proverbs and Performance in Biblical Wisdom*, Journal for the Study of the Old Testament Supplement Series, vol. 356 (Sheffield, UK: Sheffield Academic Press, 2002), 19–20.

27. See James B. Pritchard, ed., *The Ancient Near East: An Anthology of Texts and Pictures* (Princeton: Princeton University Press, 1958), 237–43.

The wisdom needed to negotiate the struggles and contingencies of earthly life has its ultimate source in God, but it is mediated through human traditions and practices. Within a wisdom ecclesiology, church life is a site of training in wisdom. To paraphrase a Reformation idiom, wisdom comes through hearing a word from outside oneself (Rom. 10:17). But this idiom may suggest a primarily cognitive process, and this obscures the pervasive wisdom emphasis on the human heart and its passions. Wisdom is finally about ordering our desires aright. The pastoral Augustinianism noted above dovetails with a wisdom ecclesiology. Indeed, according to Marcus Plested, wisdom emerges as "the alpha and omega" of Augustine's theology.[28] Augustine sees no contradiction between the desperate human need for grace and the importance of striving for wisdom, and his writings abound with appeals to biblical Wisdom texts.

As Augustine knows, the heart's reorientation toward God through communal formation is a slow and gradual process. The Wisdom books likewise puzzle over humanity's persistent attempts to live at cross purposes to God's intentions and are alert to the roles of self-deception and habit in human folly and wickedness. The tragedy of a misdirected heart is never explained, much less resolved. For Israel's sages, being "wise in one's own eyes" is the height of human folly (Prov. 3:7a). Wisdom is both within and beyond the scope of human understanding. Wisdom in any full sense of the term belongs to God, and a central part of human wisdom is to acknowledge what Martha Nussbaum calls "our necessary passivity and neediness in a world that we do not control."[29] The wisdom provided by communal teaching and practice is not adequate to turn us wholly away from sin and folly or to protect us from tragedy. Within a wisdom ecclesiology, human sin and folly, both inside and outside church, remain a stubborn and tragic dimension of earthly life. Yet church proclaims the paradox that God's power and wisdom have become incarnate in the weakness and foolishness of the cross of Jesus

---

28. Marcus Plested, "Wisdom in the Fathers: An (Eastern) Orthodox Perspective," in *Encounter between Eastern Orthodoxy and Radical Orthodoxy: Transfiguring the World through the Word*, ed. Adrian Pabst and Christoph Schneider (Farnham, UK: Ashgate, 2009), 243. For an Augustinian reading of Proverbs and Ecclesiastes, see Amy Plantinga Pauw, *Proverbs and Ecclesiastes*.

29. Martha C. Nussbaum, *Upheavals of Thought: The Intelligence of Emotions* (Cambridge, UK: Cambridge University Press, 2003), 530.

Christ (1 Cor. 1:24–25), and hence it trusts that the unity of truth and goodness present in Jesus is also worth pursuing in its creaturely life. Jesus is both the pioneer and perfecter of Christian faith (Heb. 12:2).

In addition to Calvin and Augustine, Dietrich Bonhoeffer is a vital guide to charting the wisdom ecclesiology laid out in this book. In the last years of his life, Bonhoeffer became a wisdom theologian. Though there are hints of it earlier, this theological orientation is especially evident in his *Letters and Papers from Prison* and his *Ethics*.[30] Like Israel's sages, Bonhoeffer emphasizes faithfulness in the present: Christian communities should seek to determine and follow God's purposes in the midst of the ambiguity and paradox of earthly life. "Wisdom," he notes in an outline for a devotion on Proverbs 3, "is the gospel in daily life."[31] As creaturely life for himself and for those around him became more precarious and fraught with conflict and tragedy, Bonhoeffer's theological sense of its importance and gift grew. He turned to the Old Testament with a new intensity, celebrating its emphasis on the joys and obligations of embodiment. He saw a religiosity of inwardness as a betrayal of God's call to this creaturely way of life. For Bonhoeffer, Christian faith is a matter of living in the penultimate while believing the ultimate.[32] He became increasingly convinced that his church had lost this dialectical tension, taking refuge in its liturgical and creedal traditions as a way of avoiding the earthly costs of discipleship. For Bonhoeffer, the temptation to abandon the earthly city must be firmly resisted. As he writes in a letter to his fiancée: "Our marriage shall be a yes to God's earth; it shall strengthen our courage to act and accomplish something on the earth."[33] With Bonhoeffer, a wisdom ecclesiology insists that church is called to be "a yes to God's earth," not simply as a means to some other end, but as part

---

30. In one of his letters to Bonhoeffer in prison, Eberhard Bethge reports that, thanks to the former's thoughts about happiness and blessing, Bethge is reading Proverbs, Song of Songs, and Ecclesiastes "with newly awakened senses." Dietrich Bonhoeffer, *Letters and Papers from Prison*, Dietrich Bonhoeffer Works, vol. 8 (Minneapolis: Fortress, 2010), 521.

31. Dietrich Bonhoeffer, *Theological Education at Finkenwalde: 1935–1937*, Dietrich Bonhoeffer Works, vol. 14 (Minneapolis: Fortress, 2013), 861.

32. Bonhoeffer, *Letters and Papers from Prison*, 213.

33. Dietrich Bonhoeffer, August 12, 1943, letter to Maria von Wedemeyer, in *A Testament to Freedom: The Essential Writings of Dietrich Bonhoeffer*, ed. Geffrey B. Kelly and F. Burton Nelson (San Francisco: HarperCollins, 1990), 512.

of its authentic faithfulness. It affirms what Bonhoeffer calls "the profound this-worldliness of Christianity."[34]

The Genre of Wisdom

In addition to serving as a theological source for taking the doctrine of creation seriously in ecclesiology, the biblical Wisdom books also provide a model for what this ecclesiology looks like. As I have already noted, ecclesiology is an inductive discipline, drawing on the bodily sedimentation of many years of ecclesial experience. Attempts to provide a deductive account from ecclesiological first principles tend to float far above the ground of actual church life. An ecclesiology in ordinary time, like the Wisdom books, is a distillation of corporate and corporeal experience. It attempts to remain close to the flow of daily experience. It aims at *phronēsis* (practical know-how), not *theōria*. It seeks practical wisdom for Christian living, a way of communal life shaped by convictions about God's gracious character and purposes as they have been made known in Jesus Christ. This wisdom is always situated, fallible, and revisable. David Ford notes that there "can be no human overview of it, and its pursuit is prayerful, collaborative, and transformative."[35]

This is ecclesiology in the middle tint, which painters use to cover the canvas in order to give definition and depth to the more dramatic darks and lights. As Lauren Winner muses, "Perhaps middle tint is the palette of faithfulness. Middle tint is going to church each week, opening the prayer book each day. This is rote, unshowy behavior, and you would not notice it if you weren't looking for it, but it is necessary; it is most of the canvas."[36] George Herbert's "Wise Ways of the Country Parson," with its embarrassingly ordinary ruminations on daily church life, is a folksy exemplar.[37] The primary

---

34. Bonhoeffer, *Letters and Papers from Prison*, 485.

35. David F. Ford, "Jesus Christ, the Wisdom of God (1)," in *Reading Texts, Seeking Wisdom: Scripture and Theology*, ed. David F. Ford and Graham Stanton (Grand Rapids: Eerdmans, 2004), 5.

36. Lauren F. Winner, *Still: Notes on a Mid-Faith Crisis* (New York: HarperOne, 2013), 190.

37. George Herbert, *The Country Parson, The Temple*, The Classics of Western Spiritu-

aim of a wisdom ecclesiology is not aspirational—a blueprint of church as it should be—but rather a theological account of church that pays attention to its ordinary textures and rhythms. It is a view from church kitchens and parking lots and choir rooms. A wisdom ecclesiology is rooted in distinctively Christian beliefs and practices, yet its search for wisdom is not a purely intramural exercise pursued for exclusively Christian benefit. Church's role as sage is not confined to its own affairs. God calls church to become wise in its actions for the sake of general creaturely well-being. Church offers its distinctive wisdom to a wider society and hones its wisdom against theirs.

The Structure of This Book

This book has a Trinitarian structure. Part 1 (chaps. 1–2) will reflect on the doctrine of creation, traditionally appropriated to the first person of the Godhead: these chapters draw out the implications of the church's creaturehood. Part 2 (chaps. 3–5) will offer a Christological account of church in ordinary time. There the paradox of the wisdom framework will be in full evidence: Jesus Christ, the living head of the church, is both the cosmic Wisdom, in whom all things hold together, and Mary's child. Both Christological dimensions are needed to portray church as an earthen vessel that conserves great treasure. Part 3 (chaps. 6–11) will focus on church in the power of the Spirit; it will trace characteristic modes of church life, following the arc of the Christian liturgical year. The starting point is an ordinary-time reflection called "Making New and Making Do" (chap. 6), which could serve as a motto for the whole. The modalities of this part—longing, giving, suffering, rejoicing, and joining hands—will also be familiar to those in Christian communities who do not observe liturgical seasons in a formal way. Even those who live within the rhythms of the liturgical year know that suffering is not confined to the Lenten season, and longing is not confined to Advent. These chapters aim to get closer to the lived texture of church life, not primarily from the perspective of official leaders, but as viewed from the pew. My use

---

ality, ed. John N. Wall Jr. (New York: Paulist Press, 1981). Note also the resonance between the poetic pragmatism of "The Church Porch," the first section of Herbert's collection of poems *The Temple*, and the Wisdom teachings of Proverbs and Ecclesiastes.

of gerunds as chapter titles in part 3 aims at underscoring the contrasting moods, unresolved ambiguities, and repetition of church life. While Christian theology as a whole has a pronounced teleological bent, church life has a strong circular rhythm. It is a theological mistake to make ecclesiology too linear, as if the church's story were a progressive march toward clarity and purity. The repeating cycles of ecclesial life can be seen not as frenetic inertia (even though it may at times feel that way) but as evidence of the sustaining grace of God.

PART 1

Wise Earthlings

A wisdom ecclesiology begins with the first article of the creed: "I believe in God the Father Almighty, Maker of heaven and earth." This is an unusual starting point for ecclesiology. Like the liturgical season of ordinary time, God's ongoing work as Creator receives little theological attention in most accounts of church. Creation often functions as merely a scenic background for portraying the church's significance in the drama of human redemption. A wisdom ecclesiology insists that this is not a wide enough theological purview for understanding church. As Sirach declares, God's wisdom compasses the vault of heaven and traverses the depths of the abyss, holding sway over all the earth (Sir. 24:5–6). If the doctrine of creation does not receive its due, our understandings of both God and church become narrow and distorted. Ecclesiology must begin by affirming God as Creator and church as creature.

To say that the doctrine of creation is a necessary doctrinal basis for ecclesiology is not, of course, to say that it is an adequate basis. More things need to be said about church than the doctrine of creation can supply. Taking creation seriously affects how the economic work of Christ and Holy Spirit is understood with respect to Christian communities, but it does not replace the theological centrality of Christology and pneumatology for ecclesiology. Communities of Christian faith proclaim that they have been reconciled to God in Christ and now live their lives in the time between the times in the power of the Spirit, as they lean into the new eschatological reality inaugurated by Christ's resurrection. Part 2 of this book will focus on what it means for earthly believers to be in Christ, and part 3 will focus on modes of ecclesial life in the Spirit. In both these parts, however, church's relationship to God as God's creature and church's relationship of commonality to fellow creatures remain a central consideration. A wisdom ecclesiology insists that church's creaturely identity is an ongoing divine gift, neither erased nor rendered superfluous by God's work of reconciliation and consummation.

Therefore, part 1 of this book, with its focus on the doctrine of creation, provides the anchor for all that follows. It does this in two principal ways: it establishes the gratuity of all creaturely existence, including that of church (chap. 1), and it places church within the incomprehensible vastness of God's creative purposes (chap. 2).

CHAPTER 1

Creation as Original Grace

Love is anterior to life,
Posterior to death,
Initial of creation, and
The exponent of breath.

— EMILY DICKINSON, "Love Is Anterior to Life"

What does it mean to take creation seriously in thinking about church, and what difference does that make theologically?

The doctrine of creation is what John Webster calls a "distributed doctrine" in Christian theology: it not only "occupies its proper place, but is also distributed throughout the system [of Christian doctrines], forming other doctrines by which it is in turn illuminated."[1] The doctrine of creation should ground and orient everything else Christian theology says about God's economic dealings. Unfortunately, this has rarely happened in the case of ecclesiology. In this chapter I address the ecclesiological importance of creation by underscoring the ontological asymmetry between Creator and creature, and by distinguishing an ordinary-time ecclesiology from three common theological alternatives.

---

1. John Webster, "*Omnia . . . Pertractantur in Sacra Doctrina Sub Ratione Dei*. On the Matter of Christian Theology," in *God without Measure: Working Papers in Christian Theology*, vol. 1: *God and the Works of God* (London: Bloomsbury, 2016), 7.

"Love was his meaning," Julian of Norwich declares.[2] This is as true of God's work of creation as it is of the work of redemption. God's love is creative: it generates and maintains in being all reality other than God. God created the world in loving freedom, not from any imposed internal or external necessity. God has no ulterior motive in creating and sustaining what is not God. Creaturely life is pure gift. The whole universe has its source in the One who need not have brought it into being at all. God's relationships with creatures, from start to finish, are thus gracious, reflecting God's inexhaustible generosity toward what is not God. Creaturely existence is not to be conflated with the reality of human sinfulness, and thus viewed as something to be overcome. Nor is it to be viewed as a theologically neutral "given"— awaiting the advent of grace.[3] Viewing creaturely existence in either of these ways does not do justice to God's gracious presence as Creator. Creation is best understood theologically as "original grace,"[4] or "the grace of radical dependence."[5] All creaturely life, including the life of Christian communities, has its origin in this grace; before ecclesiology says anything about church's particular being or mission, it must recognize this ultimate context.

To call creation "original grace" is an analogous usage of *grace*, which in Christian theology typically denotes God's action of self-giving in Christ or the Holy Spirit. In creating, what God gives is finite, dependent existence that is other than God. But this gift of existence also establishes the Creator's enduring relationship with creatures. The doctrine of grace is ultimately about the gratuitousness of everything creaturely. Because the relationship between God and creatures is predicated on this original grace, it is intrinsically asymmetrical. All creation depends on God for its very existence, but God does not depend on *it*. As David Burrell puts it, following Thomas

---

2. Julian of Norwich, *The Showings of Julian of Norwich*, ed. Denise N. Baker (New York: W. W. Norton, 2005), 124 (spelling modernized).

3. This is why it is inadvisable to follow the common theological division of God's economic works between *works of nature* (creation and providence) and *works of grace* (election, reconciliation, and consummation).

4. David B. Burrell, "Creation as Original Grace," in *God, Grace, and Creation*, The Annual Publication of the College Theology Society, vol. 55, ed. Philip J. Rossi (Maryknoll, NY: Orbis, 2010), 97–106.

5. Philip J. Rossi, "Creation as Grace of Radical Dependence," in Rossi, ed., *God, Grace, and Creation*, ix–xviii.

Aquinas, "the very existence (*esse*) of a creature is an *esse-ad*, an existing that is itself a relation to its source."[6] Being related to God is constitutive of the creature's identity. The reverse does not hold. God's Trinitarian life is already a perfection of "being for" the other. It is supremely fitting that in creation God's self-determination is to be the One who is "for the world." But, from all eternity, God is a God of love and communion even without the world.

Process and so-called relational Christian theologies present an alternative to this postulate of original grace by softening the stark asymmetry between God and creatures.[7] These theologies posit more ontological reciprocity between the two, seeing this as the condition for genuine relationship between God and the world, and as necessary to safeguard creaturely integrity and agency. The world contributes to God's being even as God contributes to creaturely being. Translated into ecclesiology, this construal of divine immanence suggests an interdependence of God and church that has proved tempting even to theologians who reject other aspects of a relational theology framework.

Another blurring of the God-creation distinction occurs in Neo-Platonic visions of God as standing at the top of a great chain of being, with some parts of creation in a closer ontological relationship to God than other parts. The "higher" levels of created reality serve a mediating function between God and the rest of the world, bridging the chasm between them. This approach also brings ecclesiological temptations. In this case, the temptation is to a kind of trickle-down ecclesiology that elevates Christian humanity above other creaturely reality to serve as mediator of divine presence to a world otherwise distanced from God. John Zizioulas declares that Christian theology "regards the human being as the *only possible* link between God and creation," so that nonhuman creation is brought into communion with God and sanctified through the work of humanity as the "priest of creation."[8]

By contrast, the wisdom ecclesiology that I am developing here assumes that the God-church relationship preserves the asymmetry of the Creator-

---

6. Burrell, "Creation as Original Grace," 104.

7. See, e.g., Catherine Keller, *On the Mystery: Discerning Divinity in Process* (Minneapolis: Fortress, 2008); see also Sallie McFague, *The Body of God: An Ecological Theology* (Minneapolis: Fortress, 1993).

8. John Zizioulas, "Priest of Creation," in *Environmental Stewardship: Critical Perspectives—Past and Present*, ed. R. J. Berry (London: T&T Clark, 2006), 290 (italics added).

creature relationship. Church does not occupy an ontological middle position between God and creation. Because God is not in the same order of being as creatures, God's relationship to them is at once more intimate and more comprehensive. Webster notes: "In God, absence of reciprocity is not absence of relation but the ground of limitless relation."[9] It is precisely because God is wholly other than creation that God is free to be truly and graciously present. Creatures are finite, but God's grace is not. Church exists in the creaturely grace of radical dependence on God, but God has no intrinsic dependence on church either to enhance God's own being or to mediate God's presence to the rest of creation.

This asymmetrical relationship is also the ground of church's genuine creaturely agency. Because uncreated being and created being are fundamentally unlike, creaturely agency is best secured by avoiding a zero-sum view of God's action and creaturely action. God is not on one end of the same ontological scale as creatures, and thus it is not true that the more God does, the less room there is for creatures to act. The God who creates "out of the abundance of his generosity" and not "out of the compulsion of his needs" bestows a proper creaturely integrity and freedom to act.[10] Kathryn Tanner has argued that the God-creature relationship is noncontrastive. God and creation are not in competition: God's agency is the ground of creaturely freedom and agency, not a threat to them. "God's universal, direct creative agency and the creature's utter dependence on God are compatible with talk of the creature's own power and efficacy."[11] Likewise, the church's own powers and operations are secured, not threatened, by this agential incommensurability between God and creatures.

As creature, church is graced with its own integrity and capacity for action. Its receptivity to and dependence on God is not passive. Its agency is not displaced by God's. But ecclesial agency is that which is appropriate to creaturely finitude. What God creates and delights in is finite creation—mortal, vulnerable to injury and harm—in short, radically contingent. It

9. John Webster, "*Non ex aequo*: God's Relation to Creatures," in *God without Measure*, 1:125.

10. Augustine, *The Literal Meaning of Genesis*, The Works of Saint Augustine, vol. 1/13 (Hyde Park, NY: New City Press, 2002), 3.

11. Kathryn Tanner, *God and Creation in Christian Theology: Tyranny or Empowerment?* (Oxford: Blackwell, 1988), 163.

is this creation that God values and calls good. It is this creation whose flourishing God seeks for its own sake.[12] God's gracious self-determination in creation is to establish an ongoing relationship with what is not God. By extending *ad extra* the giving and receiving of God's eternal triune life, God gives creatures space and time to be themselves, inviting creatures to respond to God in ways that are appropriate to their finite, contingent, vulnerable being. Church's finite, responsive creaturehood is the starting point for a wisdom ecclesiology.

Creation and Ecclesiology

The doctrine of creation matters for ecclesiology because it is a doctrine that "opens the logical and theological space for other Christian beliefs and mysteries."[13] Yet, as we shall see, many common ecclesiological approaches attempt to anchor church's distinctiveness by denying or downplaying its creatureliness. Contemporary ecclesiologies that stand radically opposed to each other in other respects are united in their headlong flight from the creaturely sphere. Despite their pronounced differences, they share a reluctance to affirm God's presence and power in the ordinariness of communal human life. The result in each case is an incomplete account of God's graciousness toward church. A fuller doctrine of church requires a fuller doctrine of God. Along with the grace of reconciliation and consummation, the original grace of creation is a constant for the life and identity of Christian communities, and those communities truncate ecclesial self-understanding when they neglect or deny God's creative grace.

Until the late modern period, ecclesiology was a distinctly secondary doctrine in Christian theology, derivative of more central theological topics in the divine economy. An account of church in ordinary time wants to keep it that way. A wisdom ecclesiology acknowledges the communal embeddedness of Christian perceptions of God and God's work, but it resists

12. David Kelsey describes creaturely life in similar terms in *Eccentric Existence: A Theological Anthropology*, 2 vols. (Louisville: Westminster John Knox, 2009), 1:203.

13. Robert Sokolowski, "Creation and Christian Understanding," in *God and Creation: An Ecumenical Symposium*, ed. David Burrell and Bernard McGinn (Notre Dame, IN: University of Notre Dame Press, 1990), 179.

letting ecclesiology occupy the center of Christian dogmatics. We must keep in view a fuller doctrine of God and God's economy. A wisdom ecclesiology affirms, with Letty Russell, church as "a P.S. on God's love affair with the world (John 3:16)."[14]

An ordinary-time ecclesiology operates within the larger horizon of divine grace supplied by the doctrine of creation. Correlatively, it carries with it an ecclesiological bias toward the visible, historical, and concrete. The primary referent of *church* is the creaturely community of followers of Christ spread out across time and space, never exactly delineable because of its porous and imprecise boundaries. The story of God with communities of Christian faith is nested within the story of God with the creaturely world.

This combination of an emphasis on a larger horizon of grace and a bias toward the visible and concrete provides a basis on which to respond to alternative ecclesiological approaches. Three common—sometimes overlapping—theological patterns are: (1) reducing the visible church to a delivery system for private inward transformation; (2) denying church's commonality with other creatures in its visible life; and (3) insisting that what is visible to ordinary eyes is not truly the church. I will examine and critique these three approaches in turn.

Subordinating Church to Individual Subjectivity

The first approach largely evacuates the significance of the concrete historical church. It follows the "turn to the subject" in modern Western theology, a pattern of seeking the sources of religious certainty and authenticity in individual human subjectivity. The first step in coming to know God is to look inward. In this view, the public, corporate life of Christian communities is an earthly reality alongside others. It is ordered according to creaturely patterns that have only an instrumental relationship to the church's real purpose: the transformation of the spiritual and moral lives of individuals. The organized, visible church remains external to the ends it serves. The particulars of the church's phenomenal life, including its polity and liturgy, deserve to

14. Letty Russell, *Human Liberation in a Feminist Perspective* (Philadelphia: Westminster, 1974), 158.

be judged and modified according to their perceived effectiveness in producing internal personal change. Friedrich Schleiermacher, in his *Speeches on Religion*, for example, sets aside the "tyrannical aristocracy" of the church so that "every man is a priest, in so far as he draws others to himself in the field he has made his own and can show himself master in; every man is a layman, in so far as he follows the skill and direction of another in the religious matters with which he is less familiar." As individuals "increase in religion," church becomes increasingly "of less consequence" in nurturing and communicating religious affections.[15] Under the umbrella of this general ecclesiological approach, the personal transformation for the sake of which church exists can be understood variously—for example, increasing God-consciousness, heightening social-ethical commitment, inculcating correct doctrinal convictions, or bestowing special gifts of the Spirit. In any case, the outward, public realm of church is significant only as a delivery system for the inward conversion and renewal that is the heart of Christian faith. This ecclesiological approach is largely a Western Protestant phenomenon. Suspicious of religious authority and communal bodily disciplines, it assumes the primacy of individual mind and will for achieving spiritual authenticity.[16] Christian faith is first of all about the perfection of individuals separable from community and context.

Beneath this exaltation of internalized spiritual authenticity lurk a number of treacherous cultural assumptions about race, gender, and religious identity. A central assumption is that some persons are more creaturely than others, more entrenched in the externalities of bodily common life. Individual capacity for spiritual self-realization is thus uneven, with the Western, educated, adult male Christian often assumed as the paradigm. Other persons, less rational and less capable of this self-actualization, stand more in need of the crutch provided by bodily rituals and communally defined obligations. Their less advanced religiosity needs to be more tethered to earthly realities. George Lindbeck has referred to a particularly malignant and enduring form of this internalized vision of Christian faith as "eccle-

---

15. Friedrich Schleiermacher, *On Religion: Speeches to Its Cultured Despisers*, trans. John Oman (Louisville: Westminster John Knox, 1994), 153, 160.

16. Charles Taylor is the magisterial narrator of this modern Western quest. See, e.g., *The Ethics of Authenticity* (Cambridge, MA: Harvard University Press, 1991).

siological Marcionism."[17] The religion of Old Testament Israel (and, by extension, all Judaism) is viewed as more creaturely, more tied to external bodily forms, than that of the New Testament church (and, by extension, all Christianity). The spiritual, individual character of Christian faith is a mark of religious evolution, superseding the focus on communal law and bodily ritual in Jewish life.

While there is nothing intrinsic in the ideal of internalized spiritual authenticity that requires the privileging of Christian, white, and formally educated male lives more than others, this ideal was ripe for takeover by the principalities and powers of Western patriarchy, classism, racism, and anti-Semitism. From its very inception, the modern ideal of spiritual authenticity has been corrupted by these powers, making it difficult to disentangle the ideal from its damaging manifestations. These powers have shown their cunning and persistence in infiltrating other theological approaches to Christian faith, and thus a wisdom ecclesiology cannot claim any natural immunity against them.

Recognizing its own vulnerability to these same principalities and powers, an ordinary-time ecclesiology attempts to guard against them by insisting on our common embodied creaturehood as the great leveler. Christian faith, like the Jewish faith with which it is forever linked, is bodily and communal to its core. We are who we are as individuals only in our embeddedness in a physical and social context. Rowan Williams notes that Christian life is a material life, a way of conducting public, bodily life in community. "It has to do with gesture, place, sound, habit—not first and foremost with what is supposed to be going on inside."[18] We are creatures whose orientation to the world is mediated first of all through our bodies, and our religious lives are no exception to this creaturely pattern. Everything we do spiritually as Christians has a bodily basis. Our bodies are the sites of our deepest religious "knowing." The socially established practices and structures of visible Christian communities are thus central to our spiritual formation and nurture. God redeems us as bodily creatures through communal means for communal ends.

---

17. George A. Lindbeck, *The Church in a Postliberal Age*, ed. James J. Buckley (Grand Rapids: Eerdmans, 2002), 239.

18. Rowan Williams, *Faith in the Public Square* (London: Bloomsbury, 2012), 313.

Yet, to reject the internalization and privatization of Christian faith as false and dangerous is not to deny Schleiermacher's point that Christian communities have at times functioned as "tyrannical aristocracies," absolutizing their historically relative structures and practices and wielding their power in oppressive and distorted ways. To affirm that Christian life is communally constituted does not close off appropriate critical questions about the kinds of ecclesial practices and structures best suited to nurture Christian faith.

Denying Church's Commonality with Other Creatures

The second common ecclesiological approach stands in conscious opposition to the theological "turn to the subject" and its internalization of Christian faith, but does not wholly escape its modern presuppositions. It might be called the "turn to the ecclesial subject." It retains the theological assumption that there needs to be a bridge for faith and grace to cross over, but it declares the church to be the bridge, instead of reason, feeling, or some other individual human capacity.[19] The church, not the individual, becomes the locus of God's reconciling and consummating presence, and its visible, concrete life serves as the basis for theological claims about God's character and purposes. This approach yields maximalist accounts of the church that make it the touchstone of all other theological doctrines. Rather than being a derivative doctrine into which other theological teachings feed, ecclesiology becomes their source, with the church regarded as the means and end of God's whole economic work.[20]

For this approach to work, the church must be clearly set apart from other forms of human culture, eluding the creaturely embeddedness and compromises of other human communities. This ecclesiological approach

19. In describing this ecclesiological approach, I will break with my usual practice of omitting the definite article before *church*, since the theological emphasis here is on the cohesiveness of the Christian way of life and the visible boundaries between Christian communities and the rest of human society.

20. E.g., for a view of the created world as simply the "raw materials out of which God creates his church," see Robert W. Jenson, "The Church's Responsibility for the World," in *The Two Cities of God: The Church's Responsibility for the Earthly City*, ed. Carl E. Braaten and Robert W. Jenson (Grand Rapids: Eerdmans, 1997), 4.

often succumbs to the temptation to conflate the created world and the fallen world. The world outside the church is depicted as bereft of God's presence and enthralled to violence, competition, and death. Ecclesial structures and practices are then sharply distinguished from those of other human communities: they are depicted as constituting a whole, internally consistent, exemplary way of life.[21] What this looks like varies in different versions of this approach; for example, the theological emphasis can fall on the church's structures of ministry, its liturgical and sacramental life, or its communal testimony to nonviolence. What matters is the clear distinction between the church and the world. While the structures and practices of other human communities are the product of "general cultural forces," those of the church embody "the habitus or patterns of God."[22] In the turn to the ecclesial subject, the tendency to use the world as a negative foil makes it difficult to find theological space to critique the church's life.

The welcome acknowledgment in this approach of the visible concreteness of Christian life is undercut by its tendency to an over-realized eschatology. The life of the church so fully anticipates God's eschatological reign that it transcends the ordinary dependencies and limitations endemic to creaturely life. John Zizioulas, for example, describes the church as a eucharistically constituted community freed "from the causality of natural and historical events, from limitations which are the result of the individualism implied in our natural biological existence."[23] From the perspective of a wisdom ecclesiology, this is a problematic denial of Christian communities' creaturely commonality with others. Earthly communities of Christian faith are inevitably caught up in natural and historical events, and their "natural biological existence" as creatures does not imply individualism; instead, it implies intricate connection and interdependence.

Correlated with an exaggerated distinction between the church and the world is a tendency to blur the distinction between the church and God, sub-

21. Ted Smith makes this point in "Redeeming Critique: Resignations to the Cultural Turn in Christian Ethics," *Journal of the Society of Christian Ethics* 24, no. 2 (Fall 2004): 89–113. See also the further discussion in chap. 6 below, "Making New and Making Do."

22. David L. Stubbs, "Practices, Core Practices, and the Work of the Holy Spirit," *Journal for Christian Theological Research* 9 (2004): 28.

23. John D. Zizioulas, *Being as Communion: Studies in Personhood and the Church* (Crestwood, NY: St. Vladimir's Seminary Press, 1985), 22.

verting the church's creaturely asymmetry with its Creator. Once the church is severed from its connection to other communities of creatures, ecclesial agency and divine agency threaten to become indistinguishable. According to this model, to talk about God and God's presence and agency in the world simply *is* to talk about the church. When the empirical, visible church acts, we see God acting. Stanley Hauerwas says that the church provides the "material conditions" of witness to God. The concrete life of the church, he says, *is* the very substance of God's Word made flesh in the world. "God," he says, "has entrusted his presence to a historic and contingent community. . . . It is only through such a people that the world can know that our God is one who wills nothing else than our good."[24] The church becomes an Archimedean point from which to comprehend or give a comprehensive account of God's whole being and economy.

The turn to the ecclesial subject approach replicates the contrast found in some Christologies between the humanity of Jesus and that of human creatures generally. Ordinary human creatures are interdependent: they assist each other in living out their creaturehood. Such mutuality does not apply to the human person Jesus: he enhances the humanity of others, but his humanity is not enhanced by theirs.[25] This Christological lack of mutuality and dependence then gets translated into ecclesiology, in both missional and sacramental forms: like Christ, the church exists *for* the world, not in solidarity and interdependence *with* the world. To be wholly *for* the world, the church must be raised *above* the world, transcending the dependencies of creaturely life.

In response, an ordinary-time ecclesiology insists on keeping church on the creaturely side of the God-world equation. As Creator, God is already in relationship with everything that exists. God is not absent or detached from the world, or present only as a derivative from God's presence in communities of Christian faith. Church retains the radical asymmetry of a creature's relationship to its Creator. God's life is self-perpetuating, self-renewing; everything else, including church, depends on God. Church remains planted in the earth, even as it anticipates God's promised future; its life is ordered by creaturely interdependencies as well as by its eschatological hopes. Even as it leans into

---

24. Stanley Hauerwas, *The Peaceable Kingdom: A Primer in Christian Ethics* (Notre Dame, IN: University of Notre Dame Press, 1983), 97–98.

25. I develop this point further in chap. 4 below, "Mary's Child."

the dawning of God's new reign, its visible life is sustained through complex relationships to other creatures and subject to general cultural forces. Church's relationship with other human communities is always a matter of receiving as well as giving. Church exists *for* the world in its solidarity *with* the world.

Separating the Real Church from the Visible Church

The third ecclesiological approach trades on the distinction between the true church and the church of appearances. According to this model, the true church is constituted by God, not by human traditions or actions. Constituted by the Spirit, the true church is also *known* by the action of the Holy Spirit, and thus set apart from other communities by its spiritual visibility. Ordinary human assemblies come into being through a series of cultural negotiations. They are self-assembled and self-governed. They are visible to everyone and can be adequately analyzed with the tools of history and social science. Only this ordinary creaturely dimension of church is visible to historians and sociologists. According to Karl Barth, this is not the real church (*die wirkliche Kirche*), merely the church of appearances (*die Scheinkirche*).[26] As Barth insists, "the real church becomes visible because the power of the Holy Spirit enables her to step out of and shine through her hiddenness in ecclesiastical establishment, tradition and custom."[27] The real church is visible to the eyes of faith alone. This real church exists in time because it is the "earthly-historical form of existence of Jesus Christ." To properly understand church, according to Barth, "we must eliminate all ideas of other human assemblies and societies which have come into being, partly by nature, partly by history, on the basis of agreements and arrangements. The Christian congregation arises and exists neither by nature nor by historical human decision, but as a divine *convocatio*."[28] God calls the church together,

---

26. Karl Barth, *Kirchliche Dogmatik*, IV/2 (Zürich: Evangelischer Verlag, 1955), 695, 698.

27. Karl Barth, "The Real Church," *Scottish Journal of Theology*, 3, no. 4 (1950): 338. Though Barth is a convenient exemplar of this third approach, his treatment of Christian life in vol. IV of *Church Dogmatics* has much more creaturely heft and texture than the divine unilateralism that his formal comments suggest.

28. Karl Barth, *Dogmatics in Outline*, trans. G. T. Thomson (New York: Harper and Row, 1959), 142.

and calls it together for a particular purpose: to proclaim the reconciliation of the world in Jesus Christ. The true church *exists as church* precisely in its active faithfulness as witness to Christ's salvation.

Barth had no illusions that visible Christian communities constitute some ideal society of perfect Christian disciples. He was clear that church "never has been, and never is, visible in practice as the true Church . . . the 'bride without spot or wrinkle.' "[29] According to Barth, the true church is more like an event than like a stable, enduring institution that historians and ethnographers can study: we only catch glimpses of it. "The Church *is*," Barth says, "when it takes place that God lets certain men live as His servants, His friends, His children, the witnesses of the reconciliation of the world with Himself as it has taken place in Jesus Christ."[30] Church displays its true identity *as church* only when it is faithful to God's purposes for it. The real church exists as its members stand in unconditional solidarity with each other—knowing, loving, and helping each other.[31]

From the perspective of a wisdom ecclesiology, this third approach rightly insists on church's existence as gift. It does not elide divine agency with ecclesial agency, or absolutize the historical contingent practices and structures of Christian communities. The problem with this approach is that, while it attempts to give fundamental priority to God's agency in theological talk about church, it ignores the work of God as Creator. The truth that God calls church into being does not mean that all other assemblies are self-sustaining "natural societies" devoid of God's presence. Nothing exists without God's ongoing activity and power. The Christian's special calling does not nullify church's existence as a creaturely reality alongside other creatures, living in interdependence with them; nor does it negate God's relationship with other human communities. Because of their shared reliance on the work of God as Creator, church and other communities *do* have commonalities, including the need for church, *as church*, to own up to its failings. Contra Barth, "nature" and "historical human decision" *are* constitutive elements in Christian life, because the real church is a flesh-and-blood community of God's creatures. It is not a mystical, spiritual body floating above the world of economic

29. Karl Barth, *Church Dogmatics*, IV/1 (Edinburgh: T&T Clark, 1956), 708.
30. Barth, *Church Dogmatics*, IV/1, 650–51.
31. Barth, "The Real Church," 344–45.

and political arrangements. It is not a transcendental abstraction from the historically located, socioculturally conditioned realm of appearances. Even though Christians believe that their communities of faith have been given a unique role by God to manifest the gospel of Jesus Christ, they need human "agreements and arrangements" just as other human assemblies do. In fact, they often borrow these agreements and arrangements from other groups in society, with predictably ambiguous results. The saving work of God does not circumvent the concrete realities of human institutions and practices The deepest thing that church shares with other institutions is a dependence on the original grace of creation.

Affirming a Creaturely Church

Because communities of Christian faith share in the original grace of creation, their distinctiveness from God's other creatures will always be partial, not complete. An account of church in ordinary time avoids theological maneuvers that attempt to idealize and absolutize this distinctiveness. These maneuvers include internalizing faith in individual conscience, positing a self-contained alternative community, and distancing the real church from the church of ordinary appearances. Instead, a wisdom ecclesiology acknowledges that, whatever else they are, communities of Christian faith are communities of creatures held in existence by God in dependence on other creaturely reality. God sustains their life through a complex network of creaturely means, beginning with their dependence on the earth's air, water, and soil. This creaturely interdependence continues on the level of human interactions. Communities of Christian faith are "communities of God precisely in their historical contingency and social and cultural relativism, neither despite such contingency and relativity nor to the end of escaping such contingency and relativity."[32] Christian life is a life of material connection and dynamic interdependence. There is no triumphant ecclesial transcendence over human imperfection and limitation. God's creative and redemptive purposes are worked out in the sometimes tragic ambiguities of concrete, creaturely communities.

32. Kelsey, *Eccentric Existence*, 19.

An ordinary-time ecclesiology celebrates the sheer gift of communal Christian life in this time between the times, even as it acknowledges the confusion, anguish, and incompleteness of this life. It glories in the ordinary, celebrating God's earthly means of redemption, and the part Christian communities have been called to play in the healing and renewal of creaturely life. Yet its celebration of creaturely life is oriented toward God's promised future. Christian communal existence is rooted in an earth that has been rocked by the aftershocks of Christ's resurrection. Communities of Christian faith point beyond themselves to the final realization of God's purposes for creation. They refuse to identify their earthly forms of life with this final realization. Sustained by God's love, transformed by God's grace, turned toward the hope of God's promised consummation, the pilgrim community of Christ's disciples is called to creaturely humility, solidarity, and doxology. Living into this normative vision of earthly ecclesial existence requires a slow, incremental acclimatizing to the creaturely rhythms of God's original and continuing grace.

From an ordinary-time perspective, church is a school with a very long and bodily curriculum. In this school, according to Augustine, "we learn something every day. We learn something from commandments, something from examples, something from sacraments. These things are remedies for our wounds, material for our studies."[33] The Spirit's sanctifying presence in church is a gradual, sustained disciplining of the community's creaturely capacities. This spiritual formation occurs across the lifetime of individuals and across an enormous range of human levels of understanding and responsiveness. As in any learning community, there are always relative insiders and outsiders to ecclesial life, those on the fringes and those closer to the center. Yet these are provisional designations. We should beware of assuming we know what the most important gifts are and who has them. None has attained complete maturity, "the measure of the full stature of Christ" (Eph. 4:13). David Kelsey says:

> The capacities disciplined in the power of the Spirit to become competencies for the practices in which we communally live out faithful response to God are capacities rooted in our personal bodies. They are not capaci-

---

33. Augustine, "Sermon 16A," in *The Works of Saint Augustine: A Translation for the 21st Century*, vol. 3/1: *Sermons 1–19* (Brooklyn, NY: New City Press, 1990), 347.

ties unique to persons of Christian faith that are somehow supernaturally implanted by the power of the Spirit in addition to the capacities given us by God creatively relating to us. They are all part of what we are by God's creativity.[34]

The Spirit who is the Lord and Giver of *all* life is at work in Christian communities to sanctify our creaturely capacities for responding to God's gracious presence. The earthly church never completes its journey of sanctification; its life is always *in via*.

The goal of communal Christian life on earth is growth and maturation toward fullness of life with God and with fellow creatures. There is no spiritual transformation that is disconnected from Christians' visceral connections to life and the bodily conditions of life. Christians, like everyone else, "are born into the world as creatures of the flesh, and it is through our bodily perceptions, movements, emotions, and feelings that meaning becomes possible and takes the forms it does."[35] The saving work of God in Christ is incarnational: it happens through fleshly means. Singing, standing, seeing, smelling, embracing, kneeling, falling out, washing, drinking, and chewing are all vehicles for the Spirit's transformative power. Church is the corporeal context where Christians are fed and instructed, where they practice and perform their faith.[36] In one of his charming theological speculations, Augustine suggests that God could have taught all persons individually and immediately by means of angels. Had God so chosen, all the spiritual formation every human being would need could have been obtained in this direct and effortless way. Instead, according to Augustine, God's good plan was for us humans to learn from each other, because, he says, it makes a "way for love, which ties people together in the bonds of unity, [and] make[s] souls overflow and as it were intermingle with each other."[37] God's Spirit has

---

34. Kelsey, *Eccentric Existence*, 355.

35. Mark Johnson, *The Meaning of the Body: Aesthetics of Human Understanding* (Chicago: University of Chicago Press, 2007), ix.

36. For a theological emphasis on the performative character of church, see Shannon Craigo-Snell, *The Empty Church: Theater, Theology, and Bodily Hope* (Oxford: Oxford University Press, 2014).

37. Augustine, *De Doctrina Christiana*, trans. R. P. H. Green (Oxford: Clarendon Press, 1995), 7, 9.

bound us together in the laborious and precarious curriculum of Christian growth so that we will learn at the same time to love each other. God's redemptive work happens through earthly and communal means, with all the frustrations and need for patience that this entails.

The cardinal virtues of a wisdom ecclesiology are humility, solidarity, and doxology. Church has no monopoly on the work of the Spirit, and in its engagements with others, church should avoid a pedagogical imperialism that refuses to cede the role of teacher. The intellectual ecumenism of biblical wisdom is a reminder of church's ongoing interdependence with other human communities and with all living things. When church forgets this, it risks becoming a community that proclaims but does not listen; a community that gives but is not willing to receive; a community that teaches but makes no effort to learn from others. The earthly means of grace at the center of the church curriculum are intended to draw Christians to a humble gratitude for the redemption of their creaturely life and into deeper solidarity with their fellow creatures. Following Christ is a movement deeper into flesh. Christian communal practices are to witness to the original grace of bodily life and to God's commitment to re-creating it anew in Jesus Christ.

Church has been both at its best and at its worst with respect to bodies. The enormous medical, educational, and relief mission enterprises that it has sponsored over the centuries are—whatever else they may be—enactments of Christian convictions about the goodness of finite creaturehood. Within their local fellowships, Christians have also affirmed the creaturely goodness of their common bodily life: they have broken bread together, rejoiced in each other's births, cared for each other in times of need, and mourned each other's deaths. Christian communities have done all these things, at least in part, as a faithful response to God's gift and sustenance of bodily life. Yet bodies have also been the site of church's most dramatic failures. Christian bodily practices have sometimes had the effect of excluding certain persons, and they have communicated disdain for certain bodies. Alongside the explicit curriculum of grace and solidarity in the flesh has been a hidden—and sometimes not so hidden—curriculum of bodily denigration and division, powerfully reinforced and lived out in the ordinary life of Christian communities. As the body of Christ in the world, church is a broken and diseased body that mirrors the ills and divisions of the larger society.[38] Church's betrayals of God's purposes, as well as its faithfulness to them, are lived out in the body.

Not even the most sacred and central Christian practices are immune to these betrayals. For example, Siobhán Garrigan's study of the role of Christian liturgy in "the troubles" in North Ireland reveals the ways that Eucharistic practice functioned to enact and reinforce religious sectarianism.[39] The hidden curriculum of division overwhelmed the spoken liturgy of unity in Christ. Allan Boesak has chronicled how the refusal of white Reformed Christians in South Africa to share the Lord's Supper with their black brothers and sisters led to "the acceptance, the idealization, and institutionalization of that brokenness."[40] Enshrining racial exclusion in Eucharistic practice performed and reinforced the sin of apartheid. Examples such as these could readily be multiplied, showing the danger of an exclusive ecclesiological focus on the normative intentions of church practices without attention to their concrete function. Garrigan rightly critiques "the largely unacknowledged difference between the 'is,' the 'can,' and the 'should be' of the assembly gathered at Eucharist (and, by extension, of the church as a whole) in nearly all mainstream writing about Eucharist."[41] Christian communities' bodily betrayals of their calling mean that Christian practices cannot simply be identified with God's practices. God is often hidden in the life of Christian communities of faith, and is at work redemptively—sometimes in spite of them. A wisdom ecclesiology insists on the need for an ongoing critique of church practices, without giving in to the temptation to flee or transcend church's bodily curriculum of the Spirit.

The creaturely solidarity and full-hearted praise that Christians are called to is not yet fully theirs. The structures and curriculum of the school of the Spirit remain under construction. This is cause for humility and repentance.

---

38. See Dennis M. Doyle, Timothy J. Furry, and Pascal D. Bazzell, eds., *Ecclesiology and Exclusion: Boundaries of Being and Belonging in Postmodern Times* (Maryknoll, NY: Orbis, 2012).

39. Siobhán Garrigan, *The Real Peace Process: Worship, Politics and the End of Sectarianism* (London: Equinox, 2010).

40. Allan Boesak, *Black and Reformed: Apartheid, Liberation and the Calvinist Tradition* (Maryknoll: Orbis, 1984), 89-90.

41. Siobhán Garrigan, *Beyond Ritual: Sacramental Theology after Habermas* (Hampshire, UK: Ashgate, 2004), 119.

Yet this is not cause for despair because, as Emilie Townes insists, "God is not through."[42] Communities of Christian faith forge a way of life that rejoices in this good news, even as they repent, long, and struggle. To affirm creation as God's original grace is to affirm the intrinsically communal means and ends of faith over against attempts to individualize and privatize Christian life. It is to affirm the creaturely gratuity of Christian life and the finitude of its agency. It is to affirm the profound solidarity of church with its fellow creatures. Creaturely church life is marked by dependence, borrowing, patching, confessing, reaching. Even human sin and failure does not nullify God's original grace. God's love is the beginning and end of church's story.

42. Emilie M. Townes, "'The Doctor Ain't Taking No Sticks': Race and Medicine in the African American Community," in *Embracing the Spirit: Womanist Perspectives on Hope, Salvation, and Transformation*, ed. Emilie M. Townes (Maryknoll: Orbis, 1997), 192.

CHAPTER 2

Church Looks Very Small from Here

What are human beings, and of what use are they? ...
The number of days in their life is great if they reach
   one hundred years.
Like a drop of water from the sea and a grain of sand,
so are a few years among the days of eternity.

—Sirach 18:8–10

There has been no Copernican revolution in ecclesiology. It seems that theologians are still working with a geocentric universe when they talk about church, even as the world that scientists tell us about keeps getting vaster and vaster. The rest of my account of church in ordinary time will assume an earthly context, which is fitting, given that the human members of Christ's body are biologically and genetically part of the earth community. Part of the task of a wisdom ecclesiology is to insist that Christian communities of faith truly belong to the earth. Yet it is also appropriate for an ecclesiology that takes creation seriously to take a step back and consider our unimaginably bigger cosmic context as God's creatures.

The current scientific consensus is that we live in an expanding universe, a galaxy-filled space that began some 13.8 billion years ago with the Big Bang.[1] Our own galaxy, the Milky Way, is an enormous system of stars, of

1. Some scientists now hypothesize the existence of a multiverse, an infinitely large number of universes, perhaps with different physical laws from our own.

which our sun is a single, rather insignificant member. We earthlings inhabit the third planet from the sun in our tiny solar system. Biological life on earth began approximately 3.5 billion years ago, roughly ten billion years after the Big Bang. The hominid ancestor that we have in common with chimpanzees did not emerge until only about six or seven million years ago, and anatomically modern humans emerged in Africa roughly 200,000 years ago. Human beings take their place, alongside millions of other species, as latecomers to life on earth. Astrophysicist and science communicator Neil deGrasse Tyson has dramatized the brevity of human existence within this larger cosmic story by laying out the whole history of the universe to this point over a one-year calendar. By prorating 13.8 billion years across an imaginary twelve months, deGrasse Tyson's "cosmic calendar" shows that all of what we think of as human history takes place in the last minute, of the last hour, of the last day of the universe.[2] As biologist Francis Collins observes, "God writes such short stories about humankind."[3]

Church within the Unfathomable Cosmos

Christians confess that God is the creator of all planets and stars and galaxies, even of universes beyond our ability to perceive or imagine. Yet Christian theology has often shrunk this enormous cosmic story down to a minute human story. Emil Brunner is not the first Christian theologian to conclude that "the cosmic element in the Bible is never anything more than the scenery in which the history of mankind takes place."[4] This is a drastic misreading of a biblical story that stretches from creation to new creation. William Brown insists that the "world that God so loved in John 3:16 is nothing less than cosmic."[5] God's creative activity and purposes extend far beyond human history, and even farther beyond the tiny part of human history called church. Narratives of exceptionalism come easily for Christian

2. *Cosmos: A Spacetime Odyssey* (National Geographic Television Productions, 2014).

3. Francis S. Collins, *The Language of God: A Scientist Presents Evidence for Belief* (New York: Free Press, 2006), 125.

4. Emil Brunner, *Revelation and Reason* (Philadelphia: Westminster, 1946), 33n.

5. William P. Brown, *The Seven Pillars of Creation: The Bible, Science, and the Ecology of Wonder* (Oxford: Oxford University Press, 2010), 9.

communities of faith. Acknowledging the theologically significant history of the nonhuman creation creates space for church simply to rest in its shared creaturehood.

The dynamic, unfathomable universe of which we are a minute part will not last forever. Scientists are confident that at some point our sun will exhaust its supply of fuel, making biological life on earth impossible. Life on our small planet is thus a living toward death, which is true for both all the creatures of earth and for earth itself. To borrow Ecclesiastes' image, all creaturely days under the sun come to an end, and so eventually does the sun itself. Scientists predict that the universe as a whole will at some point collapse into itself (the so-called cosmic crunch) or dissipate its energy via an increasing rate of expansion. The cosmos, despite its staggering immensity of both time and space, is finite.

Where does this grand and sobering cosmic picture leave communities of Christian faith? It reminds us of the vastness and complexity of God's creation, and of our minuscule role in it. God writes such short stories about church! Creaturely life will continue long after the human species is gone. Contra Brunner, the cosmos is never merely "the scenery" for the human story or the Christian story. Nor is it appropriate to declare the humanization of the cosmos as its God-given destiny.[6] We can rejoice in God's gifts and trust in God's promises to us without pretending to understand the whole of God's work and ways, much less assuming that we are at the center of it all. Like Job's stammering before God's cosmic questions, we will never comprehend the scope of God's creative activity.

The larger cosmic picture also reinforces how rare and ephemeral biological life is. Earthly communities of Christian faith exist as a blink of an eye in the cosmic history of the universe. Like the other occupants of the earth, "we are made from the ashes of dead stars," existing in utter dependence on an intricate network of matter and energy that makes our earthly life possible.[7] We did not put this framework in place, and we cannot change the fact that it will eventually give out. In her poem "Brute Fact," Vassar Miller wrestles with what it means to embrace the fleetingness of life.

---

6. See, e.g., P. Teilhard de Chardin, *The Future of Man* (New York: Image Books, 2004).

7. Ernst M. Conradie, *An Ecological Christian Anthropology: At Home on Earth?* (Burlington, VT: Ashgate, 2005), 28.

We love a face, a body
not for perfection of feature
or color or line, but simply
because they vanish.[8]

Earthly life is cherished not because it is perfect but because it is a precious, time-bound gift. To be creaturely is to learn to love what is beyond our ability to possess and control. For the earthly church, the only appropriate response to this radical contingency is creaturely awe and gratitude—and a commitment to the flourishing of our earthly home.

A Down-to-Earth Faith

Humility has been a dangerous virtue in Christian traditions, often and easily misused. Yet humility is called for here. A proper Christian humility takes its cue from the word's etymology and grounds us more firmly in *humus*, the soil of the earth. Humility is a fitting virtue for us earthlings: unpretentious, unpresumptuous—yet unapologetic—because it is strongly rooted in the identity God has given us and called us to. Whether and however God hosts creaturely life elsewhere, we are to give thanks for our own finite, contingent, interdependent life on earth. Our understandings of church should be *earthy*, rooted in and attuned to the patterns and cycles, the vulnerabilities and resilience, of our planet. For all its struggle and heartbreak, the creaturehood of church, like that of the creation as a whole, is sheer divine gift.

From this gratitude emerges an ecological ethic. Christians are to try to live their faith as what Larry Rasmussen calls an "Earth faith." For Rasmussen, this involves

a sense of place, a sense of community, rites and responsibilities appropriate to integral human-earth relations, an insistence that the spiritual and material are inextricable dimensions of the same reality, an awareness

8. Vassar Miller, "Brute Fact," in *If I Had Wheels or Love: Collected Poems of Vassar Miller* (Dallas: Southern Methodist University Press, 1991), 255.

of the divine presence as a presence experienced in all the powers that bear upon us.[9]

A wisdom ecclesiology calls church to repent of its indifference to earthly suffering and oppression, its selfish plundering of the earth's resources, its refusal to accept the limits of its creaturehood. The earthly church witnesses to and participates in something much bigger than itself, a giftedness and hope that far exceed its own vision and understanding.

Yet a wisdom ecclesiology also resists the temptation to romanticize our earthly context. Biological life on earth is inescapably a place of suffering and death: present life is sustained and new life emerges only through the death of other creatures. Ernst Conradie notes that "evolution through natural selection has uncovered regions of terror and torture unknown to us before."[10] This raises profound theological questions about what it means to call creation good. John Haught asks: "How could a lovingly concerned God tolerate the struggle, pain, cruelty, brutality, and death which lie beneath the relatively stable and serene surface of nature's present order?"[11] There is a creaturely ontology of violence that the earthly church is ineluctably part of, and this means that there is a persistently tragic dimension to church's creaturely life.

Alien Church, Resident Church

Church in ordinary time both embraces bodily life and its connectedness to all living things and at the same time grieves and laments the "terror and torture" endemic to earthly existence. Earthly life for Christians is marked by the biblical tension between being aliens (1 Pet. 2:11) and residents (Jer. 29:4-7) in the world God has made. As Dietrich Bonhoeffer makes clear, this is not a tension between being otherworldly and this-worldly. Both alien and resident are communal modes of "belonging wholly to the

9. Larry Rasmussen, "Sightings of Primal Visions: Community and Ecology," in *Character and Scripture: Moral Formation, Community, and Biblical Interpretation*, ed. William P. Brown (Grand Rapids: Eerdmans, 2002), 408.

10. Conradie, *An Ecological Christian Anthropology*, 47.

11. John Haught, *God after Darwin* (Boulder, CO: Westview Press, 2008), 20.

world."[12] Like the figure of Woman Wisdom in Proverbs, church appears in the thick of human life, in the daily routines and struggles of ordinary people. "The church stands," Bonhoeffer insists, "not at the point where human powers fail, at the boundaries, but in the center of the village."[13]

As resident, church claims its God-given freedom to live and act as God's creature, making common cause with God's other creatures. Sometimes the imperatives of the gospel require church to join hands with others. But Christian life is not only about gospel imperatives. The ordinary rhythms of eating and resting, working and playing, are not to be scorned, nor held up to continual suspicion—as if communities of Christian faith always had more urgent and noble duties to perform. Bonhoeffer mocks those who act "as if human beings incessantly had to do something decisive, fulfill a higher purpose, meet an ultimate duty." This represents, he says, "a misjudgment of historical human existence in which everything has its time (Eccles. 3)— eating, drinking, sleeping, as well as conscious decision making and acting, working and resting, serving a purpose and just being without purpose."[14] For the resident church, the ordinary joys of personal and communal bodily life are an end in themselves, and not to be disdained or always subordinated to some "higher" spiritual purpose.[15]

Ecclesiastes repeatedly portrays the futility of a radically purpose-driven life, and this Wisdom book can help Christian communities of faith avoid instrumentalist understandings of their creaturehood. Commenting on Ecclesiastes 3, Bonhoeffer says: "[We] should find and love God in what God directly gives us; if it pleases God to allow us to enjoy an overwhelming earthly happiness, then [we] shouldn't be more pious than God and allow our happiness to be gnawed away through arrogant thoughts and challenges and wild religious fantasy that is never satisfied with what God

---

12. Dietrich Bonhoeffer, *Letters and Papers from Prison*, Dietrich Bonhoeffer Works, vol. 8 (Minneapolis: Fortress, 2010), 364. These terms call to mind the book by Stanley Hauerwas and William H. Willimon, *Resident Aliens: Life in the Christian Colony* (Nashville: Abingdon, 1989), but a wisdom ecclesiology insists on a much deeper affirmation of the church's creaturely interdependence with others.

13. Bonhoeffer, *Letters and Papers from Prison*, 367.

14. Dietrich Bonhoeffer, *Ethics*, Dietrich Bonhoeffer Works, vol. 6 (Minneapolis: Fortress, 2005), 365.

15. Dietrich Bonhoeffer, *Ethics*, 186.

gives."[16] Whether this earthly happiness is found in an evening of beautiful music, or the success of an adult literacy program, or the bounty of a church vegetable garden, Christians should receive it as God's gift. To be hankering after spiritual ecstasies in the face of God's generous provisions for earthly life is not God's will.

However, the violence and suffering endemic to earthly life also alienate church from its own creaturely existence. The goodness and coherence of the created world do not translate into its safety or predictability for creaturely life. There is a randomness and complexity in the interplay of natural forces that make suffering inevitable. Creaturely life within such a world poses inherent and unavoidable risk, and the categories of sin and its consequences will rarely be adequate to make sense of creaturely suffering. As I have noted above, the earthly church also suffers because of sin, both its own and that of others. The vulnerability and limitations of creaturehood are not the source of sin in church life, though they can multiply the damage that human sin inflicts. Burdened by both sin and creaturely suffering, church lives as alien.

As alien, church rejects what Bonhoeffer calls "a very godless homesickness for the other world" that would distance it from this world's problems.[17] Our lot is to live as earthly sojourners and strangers, and thus to answer "God's call into this world of strangers."[18] Church is not to be indifferent to the earth's sorrows and joys; rather, it is to work hard and wait patiently for God's promised redemption. Resisting the temptations to escape to an otherworldly fantasy or to retreat to sheltered Christian enclaves, Christians should "remain in step with God" in the world, not "rushing a few steps ahead" to some vision of the consummation of God's reign.[19] Precisely when the world feels least like home, church is to embrace it and remain in solidarity with it. As Bonhoeffer insists, followers of Jesus Christ need to spurn "the devious trick of being religious, yes even 'Christian,' at the expense of the earth."[20]

---

16. Bonhoeffer, *Letters and Papers from Prison*, 228.

17. Dietrich Bonhoeffer, "Meditation on Psalm 119," quoted in Eberhard Bethge, *Dietrich Bonhoeffer: A Biography*, rev. ed. (Minneapolis: Fortress, 2000), 620.

18. Bonhoeffer, "Meditation on Psalm 119," 620.

19. Bonhoeffer, *Letters and Papers from Prison*, 228–29.

20. Dietrich Bonhoeffer, *Berlin: 1932–1933*, Dietrich Bonhoeffer Works, vol. 12 (Minneapolis: Fortress, 2009), 286.

The alien church lives in a world fractured by sin and suffering. It groans with creation for deliverance. Ecological, political, and economic problems are Christian problems, problems in which church has a stake. In faithfulness to the earth that nourishes its life, communities of Christian faith must respond. Yet the suffering and perishing endemic to earthly life will not be fully overcome by Christian efforts. "Things hoped for and reached after," Deotis Roberts observes, "always elude complete fulfillment. . . . Indeed, a Christian dies reaching."[21] In the meantime, the earthly church exists in God's creative providence—and claims its identity there. It does not pretend to know the day or hour of the ultimate fulfillment of God's purposes, much less their precise contours. For now, church gives thanks for its planetary home and strives for its own earthly flourishing and that of its fellow creatures. Bonhoeffer says that "only when one loves life and the earth so much that with it everything seems to be lost and at its end may one believe in the resurrection of the dead and a new world."[22] Christians are to claim the deep earthiness of their faith and identity, acknowledging its tragic dimensions. Without this, all our bearings for knowing ourselves and God disappear. Yet as Bonhoeffer's comment about resurrection and a new world make clear, earth is church's proximate context, not its ultimate context. The Christian attachment to earth is deep and abiding, but it is not absolute.

Church's Final Hope and Home

Christian existence is "eccentric" existence, finding its center, not in itself or in any other creaturely reality, but in God.[23] On one hand, God's grace makes it possible for church to call the earth home; on the other hand, church knows that its final home is found only in God (Phil. 3:20). Eternal life for earth's creatures is life in God. Future-oriented eschatologies such as Jürgen Moltmann's seek to resolve this tension by absolutizing the proximate context of the earth. In the fullness of God's promised reign, "the earth becomes

21. J. Deotis Roberts, *Liberation and Reconciliation: A Black Theology* (Philadelphia: Westminster, 1971), 169.

22. Bonhoeffer, *Letters and Papers from Prison*, 213.

23. David H. Kelsey, *Eccentric Existence: A Theological Anthropology* (Louisville: Westminster John Knox, 2009).

the city which holds paradise within itself."[24] Moltmann disputes the current scientific portrait of the eventual end of the cosmos, claiming God's power over the future to bring into being "a cosmic new creation of all things and conditions."[25] In his eschatological vision, the present earth will finally be transformed into an everlasting world in which there will be no death, suffering, or loss. The new heavens and earth become the site of "the immediate, omnipresent and eternal indwelling of God and of Christ."[26] For Moltmann, the Christian hope is that our proximate context on earth and our ultimate context in God eventually coincide.

By contrast, the wisdom ecclesiology that I am developing here does not understand commitment to bodily, earthly life now as dependent on the future hope for a perfect, imperishable re-creation of earthly life. Earthly life is a great but not a final gift. Christian faith does not require that the fate of our little planet be somehow wrenched out of the rhythms of the immense cosmos God has created. By God's grace, church has been given earthly space and time for living out its faith. The promise of life without suffering, pain, or death on a re-created planet earth is not required to embrace earthly life here and now. If scientists are correct, the earth and heaven we know will one day pass away. But the promises for everlasting life with God do not pass away (Matt. 24:35). This posture of living gratefully on borrowed time—within the limits, compromises, and failures of human creaturehood—nurtures an earthly life marked by both hope and longing, rejoicing and grieving. The resurrection God promises is on the other side of death: our death and maybe even our planet's death. In the meantime, there is a gratitude for earthly life, alongside an honest recognition of its fallibility and limits. Amidst the expectation that death will come, both for individual creatures and eventually for the planet, Christians rest in the hope that not even death can separate us from the love of God in Christ Jesus (Rom. 8:38–39).

For almost two thousand years, Christians have been wondering when the end will come. Of course, for the Creator of all, "one day is like a thousand years, and a thousand years are like one day" (2 Pet. 3:8). To remain in

24. Jürgen Moltmann, *The Coming of God: Christian Eschatology*, trans. Margaret Kohl (Minneapolis: Fortress, 1996), 319.

25. Moltmann, *The Coming of God*, 70.

26. Moltmann, *The Coming of God*, 315.

step with God through millennia of ordinary time requires trust that "the Lord is not slow about his promise, as some think of slowness" (2 Pet. 3:9). The expanse of ordinary time is instead an expression of divine patience with our slow progress in the curriculum of the Spirit. God has gifts that we are not ready to receive. In the meantime, we are to embrace with joy the gifts that are ours now, as they come to us from God's hand (Eccles. 5:18–20). From a cosmic perspective, the span of church's existence is "like a drop of water from the sea" (Sir. 18:10). But from the perspective of our human finitude, God's gift of time stretches out over years, centuries, and millennia, generation upon generation. Church lives within the human scale of this ordinary time, giving thanks for the space it provides to learn, grow, and hope in God's future.

The Redemption of Our Bodies

The wisdom ecclesiology sketched in part 1 argues that the doctrine of creation has not done enough work in accounts of church, and it attempts to remedy that deficit by attention to the genre of biblical wisdom. Part 2 explores how an emphasis on creation shapes understandings of Jesus Christ and his relationship to church. Since biblical wisdom traditions are the main link by which the New Testament secures the connection between Jesus Christ and creation, this will take the shape of a wisdom Christology. The aim is not to offer a full-fledged account of Christ's person and work, but instead to show how wisdom dimensions come to the fore within the framework of an ordinary-time ecclesiology.

An account of church in ordinary time insists that God's work of creation and redemption should not be set over against each other. They have different logics, in that the work of redemption presupposes the surd of creaturely resistance to God's purposes, while God's work of creation presupposes no such creaturely resistance—indeed, no creaturely existence at all. Creation and redemption thus need to be distinguished, and not conflated. They are not simply two phases of a single smooth process of God's self-giving. Yet creation and redemption both belong to the gracious work of the whole Godhead. They are both to be understood in terms of the perichoretic agency of the one triune God. There is no Marcionite disjunction between the character and work of the creator God and that of the redeemer God. Though distinct, creation and redemption are not at cross-purposes with each other, and redemption does not eclipse or subsume God's work of creation. The goal of redemption is redeemed creaturehood, not the transcendence of creaturehood. Redemption in Christ is "the redemption of our bodies" (Rom.

8:23). A wisdom ecclesiology aims to preserve this vital connection between creation and redemption.

Building on the insistence that redemption is not alien to creaturely existence, an ordinary-time ecclesiology emphasizes that the redemption of God's estranged creatures comes through creaturely means. Instead of a redemption via deus ex machina, God swooping down from above, God pitches a tent in the midst of creation. The God who creates and sustains the world from the beginning heals and transforms it from within. God works the redemption of sinful creatures from the heart of the creaturely world, through a fully human life. Thus a wisdom ecclesiology leans on the exalted New Testament declarations of Christ as God's primordial wisdom without losing sight of the portrayals in the Gospels of Jesus's authentic human-ity. This is a necessary corrective, because wisdom Christologies have often yielded portraits of Jesus Christ quite removed from the ordinary processes and conflicts of human life. In this way they risk losing the dialectical ten-sion in the biblical Wisdom books between affirmations of God's universal creative presence and attention to the dynamics of daily human existence. An account of church in ordinary time aims to preserve this dialectical tension. As the titles of the chapters in part 2 indicate, Christ, the incarnate Wisdom of God, is both the one "in whom all things hold together," and "Mary's child." Both sides of this dialectic will have important contributions to make to the concluding portrait (in chap. 5 below) of church as an earthen vessel.

CHAPTER 3

Christ, in Whom All Things Hold Together

Ages ago I was set up,
At the first, before the beginning of the earth.
When there were no depths I was brought forth,
When there were no springs abounding
with water.

—Proverbs 8:23–24

To speak of Jesus Christ is not to leave the divine work of creation behind, though ecclesiologies have often done just that, shrinking the
purview of Christology to the redemption of human existence within the
sight lines of church. A wisdom ecclesiology insists that Christ is more than
the savior of sinful humanity, more than "the head of the church" (Eph.
5:23). Christ, God's incarnate Wisdom, is the light and life of all creatures,
including those that do not sin. In Christ, according to Colossians 1:17, "*all*
things hold together." As Janet Soskice points out, "creation is always already
christological."[1] As God's wisdom made flesh, Christ is portrayed in the
New Testament as *both* the agent of creation *and* the source and pattern for
reconciled human life—the one by whom all things came into being (John
1:3) and the one through whom all things are reconciled to God (Col. 1:20).
Creation must remain on the horizon of Christology. The covenant of human
reconciliation with God does not exhaust Christ's economic significance.

---

1. Janet Soskice, "Creation and Participation," *Theology Today* 68, no. 3 (2011): 313.

The New Testament connection between Jesus Christ and creation is forged by appeals to Jewish wisdom traditions. Passages that most explicitly link Christ and creation, notably John 1:1–18 and Colossians 1:15–20, are reminiscent of passages in biblical Wisdom literature that depict the personified Wisdom of God, especially Proverbs 8, Wisdom of Solomon 6–10, and Sirach 24.[2] In Proverbs, Woman Wisdom gives a breathtaking account of herself as being brought forth at the beginning of God's ways and at God's side at the creation of the world (8:22–31). As God's Wisdom, she continues to undergird both the physical and moral order of the world: "By me kings reign, and rulers decree what is just" (8:15). In Sirach, Woman Wisdom likewise asserts her presence "before the ages" and gives an exalted self-description:

> I came forth from the mouth of the Most High,
> and covered the earth like a mist.
> I dwelt in the highest heavens,
> and my throne was in a pillar of cloud.
> Alone I compassed the vault of heaven
> and traversed the depths of the abyss. (Sir. 24:3–5)

There is no part of creation untouched by her presence. The Wisdom of Solomon describes personified Wisdom as "the fashioner of all things," God's agent at creation (7:22), and in a stunning passage goes on to declare:

> For she is a breath of the power of God,
> and a pure emanation of the glory of the Almighty;
> therefore nothing defiled gains entrance into her.
> For she is a reflection of eternal light,
> a spotless mirror of the working of God, and an image of his goodness.
> Although she is but one, she can do all things,
> and while remaining in herself, she renews all things;
> in every generation she passes into holy souls
> and makes them friends of God and prophets. (Wis. 7:25–27)

2. This is spelled out in Jean-Noël Aletti, *Colossiens 1, 15–20*, Analecta Biblica 91 (Rome: Biblical Institute Press, 1981), and Raymond E. Brown, *The Gospel according to John*, vol. 1 (New York: Doubleday, 1966), cxxii–cxxv.

It is not surprising that New Testament paeans to Jesus Christ echo these depictions of personified Wisdom. When the earliest Christians, steeped in Jewish scriptures, were looking for a way to express their faith in Jesus Christ, they found no better vehicle than the exalted portraits of Woman Wisdom.[3] What Judaism eventually claimed for Torah is claimed by Christians for Christ.

Passages such as John 1:1–18 and Colossians 1:15–20 are profound appropriations of Jewish wisdom traditions. It is important to note that the New Testament writers use these traditions selectively, since biblical wisdom does not speak with one voice. Wisdom has to do with God's ordering of the creaturely world and with God's purposes for the well-being of creation, but the Wisdom books are not equally sanguine about the effects of God's wise presence and the human ability to discern it. Ecclesiastes, for example, is convinced that God's wisdom is "far off," beyond the reach of human seeking (Eccles. 7:24). According to Qohelet, the teacher of Ecclesiastes, the patterns of God's wisdom in the everyday world are often impossible to make out. Job glories in the extravagant displays of divine wisdom in the nonhuman creation, but he confesses that "mortals do not know the way to it" (Job 28:13). Both Qohelet and Job grieve and rage against what seems to be the inconsistent presence of God's wisdom in the world.

The New Testament writers instead emphasize the strands of Jewish wisdom traditions that affirm wisdom's primordial presence and ongoing visibility in the creaturely world and in human existence, at least for those with eyes to see. By linking the divine wisdom undergirding the whole creation with the redeeming work of God in Christ, John and Colossians affirm that the disruption of the creaturely order by sin does not ultimately defeat God's good purposes for creation as a whole. In Christ, the light of God's incarnate wisdom shines in the darkness of the world's disorder and alienation, and "the darkness does not overcome it" (John 1:5). Despite their different logics, creation and redemption are both reflections of God's wisdom.

Though Jewish wisdom traditions leave traces throughout the New Testament portrayals of Jesus Christ, my focus here will be on Colossians 1:15–20. This passage articulates the grandest promise of Christian faith with poetic

---

3. See the account in Ben Witherington, *Jesus the Sage: The Pilgrimage of Wisdom* (Minneapolis: Fortress, 1994).

beauty: God, the creator of "all things visible and invisible," is at work without interruption or impediment in the life of Jesus of Nazareth. In Jesus's fully human life and death "the fullness of God was pleased to dwell." Colossians jumps effortlessly from the universality of creation to the particularity of the cross. The divine wisdom incarnated in this particular human life, with all its struggle, weakness, and ambiguity, is paradoxically the same primordial wisdom present from the beginning with God, "rejoicing in his inhabited world and delighting in the human race" (Prov. 8:31). Augustine makes this Christological affirmation succinctly by appealing to the figure of Woman Wisdom: "She is sent in one way that she may be with human beings; she has been sent in another way that she herself might be a human being."[4] The triune God's reconciliation of sinners in Christ is not a betrayal or abandonment of God's creaturely purposes from the beginning. The wisdom of the cross is opposed to the corrupt and death-dealing wisdom of the world, but not to the true wisdom of the universe. God's wisdom incarnated in Jesus Christ stretches from the beginning to the end of the creaturely story: the "firstborn of all creation" is also "the firstborn from the dead." Paradox abounds, but there is no alienation between God's creative and redemptive wisdom.

A wisdom ecclesiology claims the paean to Jesus Christ in Colossians, while resisting certain theological appropriations of it. In particular, an account of church in ordinary time rejects a totalizing interpretation of this passage that makes the incarnation "the pattern or genus in which all Creator-creature relations are subsumed."[5] This is to eclipse the perichoretic presence and agency of the triune God. The original grace of creation has its own integrity; incarnation is not the sole bridge between God and creatures. Instead, it is better to read this passage as "holding together" creation and redemption as the work of the one God. To describe God's agency in creation, the author of Colossians speaks of the eternal wisdom of God *as* the incarnate Jesus. This interpretive strategy follows the order of Christian knowing.

4. "Sed aliter mittitur ut sit cum homine; aliter missa est ut ipsa sit homo" (Augustine, *De Trinitate* 4.20.27, *Corpus Christianorum*, Series Latina [Turnhout, Belgium: Brepols Publishers, 1968], 50:197.

5. Katherine Sonderegger rejects this interpretation in *Systematic Theology*, vol. 1 (Minneapolis: Fortress, 2015), xix. In this paragraph I am indebted to Sonderegger's Christological reasoning.

For Christians, the human life of Jesus is "a spotless mirror of the working of God" (Wis. 7:26), the source of their confidence about God's character and purposes. Based on this unsurpassable, irrevocable manifestation of God's wise purposes in the incarnate Jesus, Christians can speak retrospectively of God's manifestations elsewhere, referring to God's primordial wisdom by this earthly name. God's universal sustaining creative presence is not governed by some abstract principle of cosmic order. But neither is it absorbed into the particularity of Christ's incarnation and death on the cross. Instead, the deep coherence of God's triune work of creation and redemption is affirmed. The challenge for ecclesiology is to retain this coherence.

Church and the Firstborn of All Creation

Five times in six verses the author of Colossians uses the Greek phrase *ta panta*: all things. All things have been created by Christ, through Christ, and for Christ. In him all things hold together, and through him God reconciles all things. Colossians 1:15–20 recapitulates the essential ontological asymmetry between God and creation. Church stands on the creaturely side of this asymmetry, part of "all things" that are created and sustained through God's wisdom. Christ is the divine life translated into a creaturely medium; church is not. The present tense of the verbs in vv. 17–18 is important. Christ is not simply the past founder of the church, the one whose blessed memory now inspires the activity of his followers. Colossians insists that Christ is the living "head of the church," the one who continues to hold all things together, addressing and animating the company of his followers and calling them to creaturely solidarity with all things visible and invisible.

How often church has betrayed this universal reach of Christ—or tried to claim it for itself! Theological frameworks have often shrunk the parameters of Christ's concern to the boundaries of church. The implication has been that, in Christ, "all things Christian" hold together—or even worse—that all things creaturely are held together *by* or *as* the church. Non-Christian humanity and the entirety of nonhuman creation either drop out of theological view entirely or get absorbed by God's purposes for church. Church becomes the end of the ways of God, either as the narrow focus of God's favor or as the sole channel for the continuation of Christ's mediatorial work. The vastness of creaturely time and space, the expansive promises of creation's consummation, the costly work of reconciliation and redemption—all these are oriented toward the benefit of communities of Christian faith. This particular group of creatures is posited as the chief beneficiary of God's entire economy, or else the chief mechanism through which the benefits of this economy extend to others.

This ecclesiological temptation takes many forms, but it can be seen in stark relief in the pitched battles among Reformed theologians, both in the Netherlands and within the Dutch immigrant communities of North America in the early twentieth century. The Dutch Reformed dispute was over the logical interrelationships of eternal divine decrees. Herman Hoeksema sought a clear answer to the theological questions: "What in those decrees is conceived as purpose—and what as means? What is the main object in those decrees, and what is subordinate and subservient to that main object?"[6] His opponent, Herman Bavinck, by contrast, insisted on "the manyness . . . of the decree."[7] There was, for him, an irreducible multiplicity in God's economic purposes. Thus, to a certain extent, he thought, Christian theology has to remain unsystematic, refusing to achieve a tightly unified narrative of God's modes of relating by wholly subordinating certain divine decrees to others. Bavinck put it this way: "The history of the universe can never be made to fit into a little scheme of logic. It is entirely incorrect to suppose that of the series: creation, fall, sin, Christ, faith, unbelief, etc., each constituent is merely a means toward the attainment of the next, which as soon as it is present renders the former useless."[8] But for Hoeksema and his allies, the eternal divine decrees do have a "main object," and that is the manifestation of God's glory in the salvation of some human creatures and the damnation of others. Nonhuman creation drops out of theological consideration altogether. The story of sin and deliverance completely dominates their understanding of humanity and of God's relationship to human creatures. Accord-

6. Herman Hoeksema, *Reformed Dogmatics* (Grand Rapids: Reformed Free Publishing Association, 1966), 164.

7. Herman Bavinck, *The Doctrine of God* (Grand Rapids: Eerdmans, 1951), 385. See my ecclesiological analysis of this dispute in Amy Plantinga Pauw, "Eccentric Ecclesiology," in *The Theological Anthropology of David Kelsey: Responses to* Eccentric Existence, ed. Gene Outka (Grand Rapids: Eerdmans, 2016), 91–106.

8. Bavinck, *The Doctrine of God*, 391.

ingly, Hoeksema and Cornelius Van Til, a longtime apologetics professor at Westminster Seminary in Philadelphia, categorized humanity in terms of the great antithesis between believers and unbelievers, a chasm that renders their common identity as God's creatures largely irrelevant. Hoeksema and Van Til questioned the validity of the notion of common grace, doubting whether human vessels of wrath whom God has made for destruction can be said to be recipients of God's grace at all.[9]

This industrial-strength Calvinism has dire ecclesiological consequences. By making the reconciliation of the elect the main object of God's eternal purposes, to which all else is subordinate and subservient, Hoeksema's and Van Til's theology drastically and permanently compromises the claim of Colossians that in Christ all things hold together. Indeed, even if theological attention is confined to human creatures, it is clear that, in their view, sin is the occasion for the eternal estrangement and punishment of most of humanity, striking a blow from which God's gracious purposes never recover. Their ecclesiology shrinks the cosmic scope of Christ's agency to a consideration of the ultimate blessedness of a small number of elect human individuals. Since tares and wheat are mixed together in the visible church, the circle of the redeemed is even smaller than the visible community of Christ's followers. The main object of the entire divine economy is the invisible church of God's elect. The rest of God's vast cosmos becomes mere scenery for the drama of the redemption of the elect. Within Hoeksema's and Van Til's theological framework, the purpose of church is to be a small reconciled remnant, a very partial remedy for the devastation caused by human sin, which negates the universal reach of the claims of Christ in Colossians.

Even in theologies not governed by this strict double predestination, there is a similar tendency to allow the divine work of reconciliation and the promises of consummation to eclipse the significance of Christ's role with respect to all of creation. In these accounts, Christ's incarnation is wholly defined by the work of human redemption, and church is often seen as a privileged extension of this mediating agency, its members becoming priests to the whole creation through their sacramental or missional work. Rather than take its creaturely place alongside everything else held together in Christ,

---

9. Cornelius Van Til, *Common Grace and the Gospel*, repr. ed. (Phillipsburg, NJ: Protestant and Reformed, 1995), 24–33.

church posits itself as the divinely appointed center of creaturely existence, the earthly location where God's presence is made available.

A wisdom ecclesiology, instead, follows Herman Bavinck's refusal to systematize the entire divine economy according to the single aim of human reconciliation. The insistence in Colossians that all things have been created "for Christ" (Col. 1:16) does not funnel the significance of creation into the redemption of human sinners, rendering it useless once this redemption is attained. The reconciling work of Christ does not narrow the scope of divine concern to the company of the redeemed, as if the God worshiped by Christians were only "the God of the church." Rather, a wisdom ecclesiology insists that to be in Christ is to exist in the sphere of his ongoing life and activity, which includes relationships with all things. To be in Christ is to affirm and participate in God's commitment to the whole of creation. Christ, who secures our adoption as children of God, also makes us brothers and sisters with all other human beings. In view of the universality of Christ's creative agency, Christians are to affirm their common humanity with all. They must reject any "ecclesial ontology" that might suggest that the only authentic human creatures are those baptized into the circle of church.[10]

A wisdom ecclesiology has larger creaturely implications as well: those who follow Christ, "in whom all things hold together," are not to turn their backs on any part of created reality. If in Christ they are brothers and sisters to all their fellow human beings, in him they are also "cousins to every other living being."[11] Through Christ, "God was pleased to reconcile to himself all things" (Col. 1:20), including the nonhuman creation that has been sinned against by human rapacity and indifference. Christ reveals God's purpose for humanity to include irrevocable solidarity with creation. Love of God and love of the creaturely neighbor are not opposed to each other. Dietrich Bonhoeffer declares: "God, the Eternal, wants to be loved with our whole heart, not to the detriment of earthly love or to diminish it, but as a sort of *cantus firmus* to which the other voices of life resound in counterpoint."[12]

10. See, e.g., Stanley Grenz, *The Social God and the Relational Self: A Trinitarian Theology of the Imago Dei* (Louisville: Westminster John Knox, 2001), 304–66.

11. Thomas Berry, *The Christian Future and the Fate of Earth* (Maryknoll, NY: Orbis, 2009), 84.

12. Dietrich Bonhoeffer, *Letters and Papers from Prison*, Dietrich Bonhoeffer Works, vol. 8 (Minneapolis: Fortress, 2010), 394. *Cantus firmus* is the lead melody in a polyphonic

While the immediate context of Bonhoeffer's insistence is sexual love between human creatures, his point can be extended to other creaturely bonds. Christian devotion to Christ is not to the detriment of love for "all things visible and invisible." Instead, as the firstborn of all creation and the head of the body, the church, Christ provides the foundation and model for an expansive creaturely solidarity and faithfulness.

Church and the Powers

The argument up to this point has been that church betrays Christ's cosmic significance when it denies its commonality with other creatures. My argument in this section is that it also betrays the universal reach of Christ's agency when it practices a hegemonic theology of human difference. Church is a fleshly way of being in the world. Faith comes as creatures are called, embraced, and indwelt by God. This comes through hearing (Rom. 10:17), but also through seeing, smelling, tasting, and touching. Faith is received and perceived first of all in our bodies, and God works redemptively through our bodies to create a world where creaturely bodies are celebrated and affirmed. Shawn Copeland writes:

> In solidarity, the Creator is worshipped, *humanum* honored, particularity engaged, difference appreciated. Solidarity affirms the interconnectedness of human beings in common creatureliness. Humanity is no mere aggregate of autonomous, isolated individuals. Humanity is one intelligible reality—multiple, diverse, varied, and concrete, yet one.[13]

To be in Christ is to acknowledge and celebrate this "multiple, diverse, varied, and concrete" humanity that we share in common. Therefore, church must be held to account for the ways it is implicated in oppressive divisions and invidious categorizations of this common humanity.

God's embrace of human flesh in the incarnation calls Christians to a

---

composition: it anchors the other voices. For more reflection on Bonhoeffer's use of musical analogies to describe the Christian life, see the Epilogue.

13. Shawn Copeland, *Enfleshing Freedom* (Minneapolis: Fortress, 2009), 100.

profound human solidarity. Yet Christians have often fallen hopelessly short of Colossians's universal vision of a common humanity, and have fastened instead onto the myopic distortions promulgated by the fallen principalities of the world, what Colossians calls "thrones or dominions or rulers or powers" (Col. 1:16). These are the patterns and structures that weave human society together and operate powerfully, often at an unconscious level, to define how persons and groups engage the world and each other.[14] In their fallen form, they reinforce hierarchical and oppressive forms of social relationships, which they both internalize and externally replicate. Our existence as embodied creatures cannot be separated from the operation of these principalities and powers. As Mayra Rivera notes, human "bodies inhabit a world shaped by social ideas and practices. Each body's visible traits, its place in prevailing social hierarchies, affects its exposure to the world—how a body is seen, heard, approached."[15] Rivera uses the phrase "social-material flesh" to emphasize the intertwining of the social and material dimensions of embodied creaturely life.

The sinful social distortions and denials of the reality of a common humanity have followed two main trajectories. The first trajectory disdains what is fleshly and empowers those who occupy privileged social positions to project the despised traits of flesh onto others, such as women, the poor, religious others, and sexual minorities. In the racialized world of Western modernity, those outside the paradigm of whiteness are likewise deemed more fleshly. Flesh becomes an index of weakness, of dependence, a falling short of the paradigmatic distinctiveness that sets humans apart from non-human creation. Groups of people identified with the constraints of fleshly existence are deemed less capable of rationality and self-control, thus needing to be governed and disciplined by those who are less encumbered by corporeal limitations.

The second distorting trajectory trades on a fallen aesthetic that deems only certain bodies beautiful, intelligent, and desirable. Certain paradigms of skin color and body shape and gender performance are idolized as normative for humanity. These idolized norms are not wholly constant, but vary

14. I am broadly following the interpretation of Walter Wink, *Engaging the Powers: Discernment and Resistance in a World of Domination* (Minneapolis: Fortress, 1992).

15. Mayra Rivera, *Poetics of the Flesh* (Durham, NC: Duke University Press, 2015), 133.

from culture to culture. As Willie Jennings notes, "Idols are constituted not by the particularities of their materiality but by their trajectories, which are aimed at prescribing the universal."[16] In the modern context, Jennings laments the dominion of a "pigmentocracy" in which "color caste systems permeate economies of beauty, ecologies of assessment, and the dreamscapes of people."[17] Sexual minorities and those with disabilities find similar caste systems in place.

The creaturely church lives in the ambiguity of the penultimate, in which the principalities and powers are still operative. It is "torn on the horn between season and season, time and time, between hour and hour, word and word, power and power."[18] The company of Christ's followers inhabits a social space that is being drawn into God's true life of reconciliation and communion. But church is also a space that remains estranged from the new identity it claims in Christ, and in fact often appears to be in league with the fallen thrones and dominions. This is particularly clear in Christian theologies that attempt to prescribe the "natural order" of things, whether that concerns political structures, racial differences, or relationships between men and women. These varied attempts at delineating so-called natural orders of creation commonly end up replicating the cycles of violation and oppression found in reigning structures and institutions of the host society. Even the author of Colossians signs on to the enthroned system of Greco-Roman family values, in which women are subject to men, slaves obey masters, and the roles and authority of human masters and God are so conflated that the same word is used to refer to both (Col. 3:18–4:1). With anguish, Christians confess that church has often played host to the fallen powers, becoming a site where certain bodies are denigrated, subordinated, and excluded. It has ordered its life around distorted visions of social-material flesh. In so doing, church has failed to affirm the true character of Christ's dominion. It has shortchanged the life-giving scope of Christ's rule.

16. Willie James Jennings, "The Aesthetic Struggle and Ecclesial Vision," in *Black Practical Theology*, ed. Dale P. Andrews and Robert London Smith Jr. (Waco, TX: Baylor University Press, 2015), 181; see also Willie James Jennings, *The Christian Imagination* (New Haven, CT: Yale University Press, 2010).

17. Jennings, "The Aesthetic Struggle," 180.

18. T. S. Eliot, "Ash Wednesday," in *Collected Poems 1909–1962* (Orlando, FL: Harcourt, Brace, 1963), 83.

Peace through His Blood

In confessing their betrayals of the Christ in whom all things hold together, Christians gather around the humiliated, tortured body of Jesus. His promise of reconciled life in communion with all things is hidden in the turbulent flow of human history, because the event that establishes this new way of life "looks for all the world like a triumph for the forces of violence and disorder."[19] Christ draws us into this new common life through his death, "making peace through the blood of his cross" (Col. 1:20). Being a community that lives into this peace is at the heart of church's calling, a calling that is inseparable from an ongoing confession of its failures. Acknowledging guilt toward Christ is church's only way forward. Indeed, as Bonhoeffer declares, "it is tautological to say that the church is the place where guilt is acknowledged." Church simply is "that community of people that has been led by the grace of Christ to acknowledge its guilt toward Christ."[20]

In this acknowledgment of the intermingling of guilt and grace in Christian life, a wisdom ecclesiology insists that the remedy is not to abandon the ordinary material practices of church. There is no purity to be had in a flight to disembodied spiritual inwardness; nor is there unity in Christ achieved by pretending to transcend the concreteness of bodily particularity. In its rejection of distorted versions of "natural theology," church should not retreat to a Gnosticism that spurns the sphere of the natural, that is indifferent to the bodily, physical, communal dimensions of creaturely existence. Christ's grace and power are present in the public and visible worship, witness, and reflection of his followers, even if this grace and power is also at work outside church and sometimes in spite of church. For Christ there is no straight line from being the firstborn of all creation to being the firstborn from the dead (Col. 1:15, 18): in between come suffering and death. In an analogous way, there is no straight line from earthly church practices and structures to the resurrection life of God's reign. Church's way forward is not a matter of simply perfecting or fulfilling the potential of its current form of life.

19. Richard Bauckham, "Where Is Wisdom to Be Found? Colossians 1:15-20 (2)," in *Reading Texts, Seeking Wisdom*, ed. D. F. Ford and G. Stanton (London: SCM, 2003), 135.

20. Dietrich Bonhoeffer, *Ethics*, Dietrich Bonhoeffer Works, vol. 6 (Minneapolis: Fortress, 2005), 135.

Church must also be willing to undergo the mortification and death of its sinful ways in order to find new earthly ways of life in the Spirit. God calls church to be a pilot project for creaturely flourishing. Grounded in Christ, in whom all things hold together, church reaches for new life beyond all the diminishments of our joint creaturehood by centuries of division and alienation. Christ's Spirit propels church toward the other, toward a universal communion of lives woven together in love for God and each other.

CHAPTER 4

Mary's Child

Born in the night, Mary's Child,
a long way from your home;
coming in need, Mary's Child,
born in a borrowed room.

—GEOFFREY AINGER,
"Born in the Night, Mary's Child"

The preceding chapter noted that Colossians 1:15–20 spans the universal and the particular: it links the primordial and ongoing creative work of God with the story of Jesus's death on a cross in first-century Palestine. Christ, the one in whom all things hold together, is also the son of David, Mary's child. The divine wisdom incarnated in this particular human life and humiliating death does not eclipse or contradict the primordial wisdom by which all things were made. The triune God is graciously at work in both. Augustine praises God that the "Word became flesh so that your Wisdom, through whom you created all things, might become for us the milk adapted to our infancy."[1] Yet these manifestations of God's wisdom should not be seen as a natural progression, a smooth unfolding of a single divine logic. The modulation from creation to cross is jagged and dissonant. To affirm the cross as a manifestation of God's wisdom is a deeply paradoxical movement.

---

1. Augustine, *Confessions* 7.24, trans. Maria Boulding (Hyde Park, NY: New City Press, 2001), p. 178.

Scripture is an intricate tapestry of revisions, retellings, and reappropriations: it is a text in conversation with itself. Some of the links in this conversation are easy to follow, such as those between the exalted self-descriptions of Woman Wisdom and the cosmic depiction of the Word in the prologue of John's Gospel. However, wisdom is a way of seeing that goes below the surface to open up space for the unexpected and subversive. In the New Testament writers' wrestling with the drama of Jesus's suffering and death, the appropriations of Woman Wisdom are bent and made strange. Proverbs 3:16–17 declares: "Long life is in her right hand; in her left hand are riches and honor. Her ways are ways of pleasantness, and all her paths are peace." In the Christological retellings, Woman Wisdom's frank associations with security, wealth, and social status are stripped away. It is at the cross, at the point where Jesus's human struggles and risks look like only weakness and foolishness, that the apostle Paul proclaims "Christ the power of God and the wisdom of God" (1 Cor. 1:23–24).

Wisdom Christologies have often shied away from this paradox, preferring a cosmic Christ who transcends the messy particulars of Jesus's human life. Attempts to connect Jesus and the biblical figure of Woman Wisdom have often come at the cost of affirming Jesus's full humanity. Contemporary wisdom Christologies have taken a bewildering variety of forms—Christ as laconic sage, avatar of universal divine wisdom, eternal ordering principle of the universe, to name only a few—and remain a subject of sharp disagreements among biblical scholars and theologians. However, it is fair to say that from the early church onwards, wisdom Christologies have often yielded portraits of Jesus Christ that are distanced from the ordinary processes and conflicts of human life. This tendency to abstraction is reflected even in depictions of Jesus as an earthly sage. In the noncanonical gospels, such as the Gospel of Thomas, and in the contemporary portrayals of Jesus indebted to them, Jesus's wisdom seems quite disengaged from the political and social context of first-century Palestine. Jesus appears as a sage who dispenses generic human wisdom that transcends the specificities and limitations of his context.

An ordinary-time ecclesiology cannot afford this abstraction. It will instead follow the perplexities of the canonical portrayals of Jesus and their sometimes brutal realism about what it means for God to assume a fully human life. Attention to Jesus as Mary's child echoes biblical Wisdom literature's concern with what the divine wisdom that anchors all things looks like in the dynamics and difficulties of daily human life. As we shall see, attention to the vulnerabilities and limitations of Jesus's earthly life provides guidance for negotiating the dynamics and difficulties of church life and helps guard against triumphalist or escapist temptations.

Jesus's way in the world is the way of renunciation. "Not regarding equality with God something to be exploited, he emptied himself, taking the form of a slave" (Phil. 2:6-7). The "emptying" (*kenōsis*) involved in the incarnation is not a matter of abandoning or setting aside divine attributes in order to take up human ones. This emptying is instead the most authentic manifestation of God's power and grace. Gregory of Nyssa observes that God's "transcendent power is not so much displayed in the vastness of the heavens or the luster of the stars or the orderly arrangement of the universe or his perpetual oversight of it, as in his condescension to our weak nature."[2] God's power and grace *are*, of course, displayed in the "vastness of the heavens" and in God's "perpetual oversight" of all creatures great and small. The original graciousness of God's creative work is not contradicted or nullified in the incarnation of God's wisdom in Jesus Christ. Christ's incarnation is the intimate and costly divine embrace of the creaturely matter God continues to create and uphold in being.

A Truly Human Savior

Jesus is Mary's child. In whatever way we understand Mary's conception of Jesus, he is her child by a fully human birth. Still, given human ambivalence about life in the flesh, it is not surprising that there is a long history of Christian theological attempts to deny the real human birth and flesh of Jesus. Bodily existence is the source of both our deepest joys and our deepest pain and sorrow, and both of these extremes—and all the ordinary life in between—can seem unworthy of God's intimate indwelling. Appealing to the dichotomous biblical language in passages such as John 3:6 ("what is born of the flesh is flesh, and what is born of the Spirit is spirit"), some

2. Gregory of Nyssa, *Address on Religious Instruction* 24, trans. Cyril C. Richardson, in *Christology of the Later Fathers*, ed. E. R. Hardy (Philadelphia: Westminster, 1954), 301.

Christian theologians have concluded that the infant Jesus did not take his fleshly body from Mary, but rather received heavenly flesh from God. In their understanding, human flesh is alienated from God and tainted by sin, and this taint is passed down as a kind of toxic genetic inheritance. If Jesus's body had truly come from the flesh of Mary, then Jesus would be a sinner by birth, incapable of extending salvation to others born of the flesh. Jesus must thus be exempted from this origin in sinful flesh. This can happen either by setting Mary's humanity apart from ordinary sinful humanity (though that seems simply to move the problem back a generation) or by positing that Jesus was not really Mary's child. According to this second line of reasoning, Jesus slipped through Mary uncontaminated, like water through a pipe.[3] Rather than assuming genuine human flesh, God's Wisdom is miraculously transformed into a human being within the womb of Mary. Menno Simons says, "He did not become flesh *of* Mary, but *in* Mary."[4] Despite the soteriological concerns driving the denials of Jesus's fully human birth, any theological proposal that makes the flesh of Jesus essentially unlike other human flesh sabotages human salvation. Only what is united with God can be saved: "That which Christ has not assumed he has not healed."[5] Better to say, then, that the humanity assumed by God in Jesus is ordinary, fallen humanity, and that Jesus was Mary's child by a truly human birth.

Jesus's human journey began, like all human journeys before the advent of modern medicine, in the darkness of a maternal womb. From zygote to floating blastocyst to an embryo implanted in the lining of Mary's uterus, Jesus's earliest human beginnings were hemmed in by the limits and dependencies of creaturely existence. The "firstborn of all creation" begins human life in a pool of endometrial blood, "a re-creation not from nothing, but from everything, from the universal stuff of life."[6] Elizabeth Gandolfo reminds us

---

3. This image comes from the sixteenth-century Anabaptist Melchior Hoffmann; see Klaus Depperman, *Melchior Hoffman*, trans. Malcolm Wren (London: T&T Clark, 1987), 215.

4. Menno Simons, "Brief Confession on the Incarnation (1544)," in *The Complete Works of Menno Simons*, ed. J. C. Wenger (Harrisonburg, VA: Herald Press, 1956), 432 (italics added).

5. Gregory of Nazianzus, "To Cledonius the Priest against Apollinarius (Letter 101)," in *Nicene and Post-Nicene Fathers*, second series, ed. Philip Schaff (Peabody, MA: Hendrickson Publishers), 7:440.

6. Elizabeth Gandolfo, "A Truly Human Incarnation: Recovering a Place for Nativity in Contemporary Christology," *Theology Today* 70, no. 4 (2013): 383.

that the "liberating good news of divine incarnation does not begin with Jesus's public ministry as an adult. Rather, it begins with a socially high-risk pregnancy; with a humble, messy, and painful birth, and with the natal body of a squalling, dependent, and vulnerable infant."[7] Christmas-card sentimentality of a serene mother and baby glosses over the pain and riskiness of a real human birth, the utter dependence of a newborn on food and warmth and care. In Christ, God comes to us not first as a teacher and savior, but as a hungry child. To be a human creature is to receive our flesh from another. That is what Jesus's birth as Mary's child affirms.

What we receive at birth is more than a biological connection to our mother's flesh. Birth places us in the tangled network of human relationships—familial, economic, political, cultural. These, too, are inherited, not chosen, and they shape the contours of our human life from the beginning. As Howard Thurman spells out in his classic *Jesus and the Disinherited*, it makes a profound difference that Jesus was born and lived as a poor Jew in a land occupied by an imperial power.[8] The weakness of the flesh is not simply biological. To embrace a fully human life is to embrace the social vulnerabilities and dependencies that accompany it.

A human birth is a new chapter in a very long story. Jesus's human life derives not just from Mary. Through her it reaches back to the whole house and family of David. Jesus is also flesh of their flesh, bone of their bone. As Tertullian affirms, "the flesh of Christ adheres not only to Mary, but also to David through Mary and to Jesse through David."[9] Through Jesus's flesh, the story of church is linked forever to the story of Israel. The genealogy in Luke's Gospel traces Jesus's lineage all the way back to Adam, the original human earth creature, made by God from the dust of the ground. Sharing Mary's flesh establishes bonds that go all the way back to this dust. The amniotic sea of Mary's womb is linked to the primeval seas of the planet earth and ultimately to the very beginnings of the universe. Jesus as Mary's child is both star stuff and earth stuff: his is a "deep incarnation," going to the heart of material reality.[10]

7. Gandolfo, "A Truly Human Incarnation," 384.

8. Howard Thurman, *Jesus and the Disinherited* (Boston: Beacon Press, 1976).

9. Tertullian, *Tertullian's Treatise on the Incarnation* 21, trans. Ernest Evans (London: SPCK, 1956), 73.

10. Niels Gregersen, "The Cross of Christ in an Evolutionary World," *Dialog: A Journal of Theology* 40 (2001): 192–307.

Christian theologians who are frank about the lowly ordinariness of Jesus's human birth typically use this affirmation to magnify the power and love of God on display in the work of human redemption: "the glory of God shining in the weakness of the flesh."[11] Their theological emphasis is on how Christ's assumption of our human nature lifts and elevates all humanity. Athanasius compares it to the honor and attention ordinary people receive when a king lives in their city. Gregory of Nazianzus likens the incarnation to the way the sun's heat burns off the morning fog and makes all the air crisp and bright.[12] Incarnation is the supreme act of condescending love taken for the benefit of human sinners. It forever changes what it means to be human. Christ is the supreme giver of gifts, the one who purifies our human nature and unites it with God.

Jesus as Creature

A wisdom ecclesiology deepens and complicates this emphasis on the significance of the incarnation by paying attention to the Gospel narratives' portrayals of the dependence and conflict that run through Jesus's life. It is not enough to portray Mary's child as the giver of gifts; to be human is also to be a receiver of gifts. Jesus's creaturely life is marked by profound interdependence with fellow creatures, both human and nonhuman. Here theologians who are focused solely on Christ's reconciling work tend to stumble. Instead of affirming the dependent character of Jesus's full humanity, they replicate the essential asymmetry between God and creatures in their accounts of Christ's earthly life. Jesus gives, but he does not receive. The result is a truncated account of Jesus's humanity and, as extrapolated to ecclesiology, a dangerous and illusory model for church.

According to Karl Barth, for example, what distinguishes Jesus from other human creatures is his lack of dependence. Human creatures as such are bound up in relationships by which they both assist and are assisted by

---

11. Irenaeus, *Against Heresies* 5.3, in *The Ante-Nicene Fathers*, ed. Alexander Roberts and James Donaldson (New York: Charles Scribner's Sons, 1903), 1:529.

12. Athanasius, "On the Incarnation of the Word," in *Christology of the Later Fathers*, ed. and trans. E. R. Hardy (Philadelphia: Westminster, 1954), 63; Gregory of Nazianzus, *Theological Orations* 30.6, in *Nicene and Post-Nicene Fathers*, 7:311.

one another in the realization of their proper creaturely humanity. In Barth's words, "The minimal definition of our humanity, of humanity generally, must be that it is the being of the human in encounter, and in this sense the determination of humanity as a being with the other."[13] To be God's human creature is to be "able and ordained to render assistance to fellow creatures and to receive it from them."[14] According to Barth, however, such mutuality does not apply to the human being Jesus: he enhances the humanity of others, but his humanity is not enhanced by them. "God alone, and the man Jesus as the Son of God, has no need of assistance, and is thus able to render far more than assistance to humanity, namely, to represent them. For us, however, humanity consists in the fact that we need and are capable of mutual assistance."[15]

Barth's portrait of Jesus cannot be reconciled with the Gospel accounts, which depict Jesus as needing and receiving assistance from others, starting with his infancy and continuing on through his adulthood. In contrast to the sin and alienation of human life that Jesus takes on in order to heal them from within, the dependence and receptivity of his earthly life are part of the way he models the Trinitarian life in which we are to participate. Barth's concern to affirm Christ's reconciling work on our behalf leads him to deny, in the case of Jesus, the mutuality that is at the heart of creaturely existence. By contrast, a wisdom ecclesiology insists that Jesus is *for* others only as he is *with* others, and dependent on them. Jesus thereby shows what union with God in human form looks like. He shows this union not only in acting to share God's good gifts with others but also in living himself in grateful dependence on God's gifts mediated through creaturely channels.

In the Gospel stories of Jesus's ministry, his dependence on others is everywhere implicit, though it rarely surfaces. There are tantalizing hints about the women who "used to follow him and provided for him when he was

---

13. Karl Barth, *Church Dogmatics*, III/2, trans. Harold Knight, G. W. Bromiley, J. K. S. Reid, R. H. Fuller (Edinburgh: T&T Clark, 1960), 247. All quotations from *Church Dogmatics* in this chapter modify the male language of the original English translation. I develop this argument further in "Christ, the Receiver of Gifts," in *The Gift of Theology: The Contribution of Kathryn Tanner*, ed. Rosemary P. Carbine and Hilda P. Koster (Minneapolis: Fortress, 2015), 81–98.

14. Barth, *Church Dogmatics*, III/2, 262.

15. Barth, *Church Dogmatics*, III/2, 262.

in Galilee" (Mark 15:40; see also Luke 8:2–3). There are undoubtedly many stories of this provision left untold that would enrich our understanding of Jesus; but clearly he depends on others from his birth onwards. The bread he blesses was baked by others. The wine for which he gives thanks was made from grapes that others grew and crushed and fermented. Even as he feeds and heals others, his own body is being nourished by the plants and animals he eats. To be human is to depend on other creatures, to receive from them. Though Proverbs and Sirach can wax overconfident about the earthly benefits of following Woman Wisdom, it is clear that human attempts to be wise are not an escape route from the vulnerability and dependence that are intrinsic to creaturehood. Jesus lives wisely by embracing the creaturely dependence and mutual assistance required for human existence.

An account of church in ordinary time insists that God constitutes in Jesus a life that is genuinely creaturely, shaped by limits of particularity and temporality, which include dependence and the need for intellectual and moral growth. According to Luke 2:52, "the boy Jesus increased in wisdom and in years, and in divine and human favor." What does it mean for Jesus, God's Wisdom incarnate, to *increase* in wisdom and in favor with God? As Kathryn Tanner articulates the doctrine of Christ's anhypostatic humanity, "the assumption of Jesus' humanity by the Word is the immediate source of his whole human life."[16] Yet the incarnation is not an epiphany, a sudden and effortless transformation of creaturely reality. Tanner avoids ahistorical construals of this humanity by noting that, while "God's making the humanity of Jesus God's own is an all or nothing affair . . . what is assumed and its effects on human life are not."[17] The entire course of Jesus's life is included in God's assumption of his humanity, but only as it gradually unfolds across the limits of creaturely existence. He was *made* perfect through sufferings (Heb. 2:10). This historical unfolding reflects the ambiguities and precariousness of all human growth and maturation. The Gospels portray Jesus as someone who was tempted, who grieved, who learned from the Syro-Phoenician woman, who was anxious before death, and who endured the agony of dereliction on the cross. As Tanner insists, "the purification and elevation of the human in Christ is a historical process because the humanity assumed by the Word

16. Kathryn Tanner, *Jesus, Humanity and the Trinity* (Minneapolis: Fortress, 2001), 16.
17. Tanner, *Jesus, Humanity, and the Trinity*, 27.

is historical. . . . Jesus does not overcome temptation until he is tempted. Jesus does not heal death until the Word assumes death when Jesus dies."[18] Not only does his wisdom and favor with God increase, the salvation Jesus extends to humanity increases as the effects of his union with the Word are realized across the various events of his life.

But even Tanner's historicized account seems to minimize the tragic dimensions of the incarnation. Temporal existence involves not only dependence on others and the need for physical, moral, and intellectual development; temporality is also a burden that compromises our relations with others. Donald MacKinnon suggests that "it is a manifest weakness of much traditional Christology that it has evacuated the mystery of God's self-incarnation of so much that must take time, that must be endowed with the most pervasive forms of human experience, its successiveness, its fragmentariness, above all its ineluctable choices, fraught equally inevitably with tragic consequence."[19] Jesus has no refuge from the perplexing limitations of temporal human life: to minister in one place is to be absent from another; to cure those who are thrust into his field of vision is to ignore others; to take time away to pray is to leave teaching the crowds for another day.

Jesus also enters into the radical and appalling contingency of finite historical agency, in which there is a persistent disconnection between our intentions and their consequences, and in which our very existence is inevitably a source of injury and risk to others. The Gospel writers sound this tragic note right from the beginning of Jesus's story. Matthew presents the birth of Jesus as the occasion for Herod's fear and rage, which results in his command for the slaughter of the innocents (Matt. 2:16–18). Simeon's blessing of Mary and Joseph in Luke includes the prophecy that their newborn child will be a source of conflict and heartbreak. Jesus is destined from birth to provoke division in Israel. His suffering will be a sword that pierces the heart of his mother Mary (Luke 2:34–35). As Rowan Williams notes, Jesus's "innocence or sinlessness becomes a dauntingly complex matter if it is not to be taken as a complete alienation from the realities of temporal existence."[20]

18. Tanner, *Jesus, Humanity, and the Trinity*, 27.

19. Donald MacKinnon, "The Evangelical Imagination," in *Philosophy and the Burden of Theological Honesty: A Donald MacKinnon Reader*, ed. John C. McDowell (New York: T&T Clark, 2011), 196.

20. Rowan Williams, *On Christian Theology* (Oxford: Blackwell Publishers, 2000), 157.

The tragic dimensions of Jesus's human life culminate in his shameful public death as a political prisoner, alienated from his religious community and abandoned by his closest followers. Betrayal, pain, and grief are integral to Jesus's story, and they must not be papered over by a triumphalist narrative of resurrection victory. Resurrection does not negate or justify the suffering of the cross. The tension between failure and triumph, grief and joy, is integral to Jesus's story, and that tension must be retained in attempts to tell church's story.

Jesus's Works of Power

Tragedy and conflict are, of course, not the only themes in Jesus's life. There are also moments of grace-filled wonder and swelling gratitude for God's gifts. Jesus was a person around whom extraordinary things happened. He was a healer and an exorcist whose renown drew large crowds of desperate and suffering people. The Gospel accounts portray him as intent on responding to the bodily needs of others. Jesus heals earthly suffering by earthly means: touch, spittle, spoken word. He feeds hungry multitudes, cures those afflicted and ostracized by disease and mental illness, even raises people from the dead. His "signs and wonders" (Acts 2:22) are not simply displays of arbitrary divine power, but instead flow from a deep sense of human solidarity and compassion. Where that human connection and trust are absent, Jesus's capacity for these acts seems stymied. Mark's Gospel notes Jesus's inability to perform significant signs in the face of his fellow Nazarenes' rejection and mockery (Mark 6:5). Jesus's extraordinary works are not stand-alone occasions for wonder. Rather, they point ahead of themselves to the resurrection and the full sharing in God's life that it promises.

Jesus's acts of healing and feeding do not mean that the earthly constraints of his creaturely life simply cease to apply. Even in the large crowds gathered around Jesus, some remained hungry, sick, and ostracized. The multitudes he feeds on the hillside will be hungry again the next day. The widow's son, whom he raises from the dead in an outpouring of compassion (Luke 7:11–15), will again face death. Most significantly, the Gospel accounts depict Jesus as refusing the temptation to perform signs and wonders on his own behalf, to ease his physical suffering in the wilderness or to come down from the cross. His extraordinary acts are evidence of his concrete earthly solidarity with others, not a suspension of it.

Signs and wonders, whether performed by the earthly Jesus or in the power of his Spirit after the resurrection, are accent notes in a wisdom ecclesiology.[21] They are not the main melody of redemption. They are to be welcomed, but not expected. Most of the time the divine work of redemption is characterized by what Tim Gorringe calls "the slow and patient pedagogy of God's Spirit."[22] Its results are not usually dramatic and immediate. Like the incarnation, our transformation into Christ's glorious image (2 Cor. 3:18) is a historical process. It takes time. The Gospels portray Jesus as a wisdom teacher who taught in parables, bringing his hearers to new knowledge of God through their shared sensible world of fig trees, sparrows, and workers in the vineyard. Likewise, the Spirit conforms us to the risen Jesus within the ordinary world in which our identity as social, embodied creatures is situated and constituted. God's saving work takes place in community—within the contingencies and limitations of creaturely life. God's redemption is an achingly difficult and slow process because it aims at nothing less than bringing all creation into joyful, eternal fellowship with its Creator. Church lives in this time between the times, claiming the fundamental hopefulness of life in the Spirit of the risen Christ and glimpsing its promise and joy, while still enmeshed in the vulnerabilities and constraints of creaturely life.

The Gospel accounts of Jesus's works of power reflect the paradox that God's transforming grace is both mediated by earthly bodies and at the same time not confined by them. Jesus's works of healing, feeding, and exorcism are cracks in the foundation of the regime of powers and principalities, in which marginalized people suffer and suffering people are marginalized, in which embodiment for so many is experienced as a terrible burden and a source of pain. Social-material existence is a gift, and the medium for our communion with God and each other. Yet we often experience the vulnerabilities and limitations of this existence as an obstacle to this intimate communion. Hunger, disease, violence, and death separate and alienate us from

21. Mark 13:22, John 4:48, 2 Thess. 2:9, and Rev. 16:14 reflect the New Testament ambivalence about signs and wonders. In themselves, they do not distinguish Jesus from other wonder workers.

22. Timothy Gorringe, *Redeeming Time: Education through Atonement* (London: Darton, Longman and Todd, 1986), xv.

each other and can constrict our trust in God's merciful presence. Even more benign factors, such as geographic distance and cultural and linguistic barriers, often impede communion. Jesus's works of power are glimpses of the promise that all the features of bodily life that stunt communion and hinder creaturely flourishing will be transformed. In this way Jesus's extraordinary acts point far beyond first-century Palestine and ahead to resurrection life. John's Gospel tells us that even the locked doors of a house do not prevent the risen Jesus from standing among his disciples (John 20:26; see also Luke 24:36). So also, the walls of hospital rooms and prisons, even the walls of Christian sanctuaries, cannot ultimately separate us from each other, or from the love of God in Christ Jesus (Rom. 8:35–39). Church is a community that trusts this promise of Christ's unimpeded presence, and by the power of Christ's Spirit, it lives as his body in the world.

Church as Mary's Child

Chapter 3 emphasized the universal reach of Christ's creative work, and how this exerts critical leverage on Christian attempts to shrink the boundaries of Christ's presence. In Christ *all* things hold together, and church is to be a community that rejects the regimes of isolation that divide and alienate. This chapter emphasizes the vulnerabilities and limitations of Christ's incarnate life and how they provide a pattern for the life of his followers. In this connection we will examine what has become a popular notion in Anglo-Catholic circles: church as the extension of the incarnation. From the vantage point of an ordinary-time ecclesiology, this is a dangerous concept, easily misunderstood. Attention to the doctrine of creation highlights the pitfalls of this ecclesial metaphor.

As I have noted earlier, a wisdom ecclesiology rejects the attempt to align all Creator-creature relations with the pattern of the incarnation. Making the incarnation the template for all God's ways flattens the variegated landscape of God's triune economy. When applied to ecclesiology, it can suggest "a biological and hypostatic" union between Christ and church as his body, which may lead to "an unhealthy divinization of the Church."[23] Applying this

---

23. Avery Dulles, *Models of the Church* (New York: Doubleday, 1974), 51.

incarnational template to ecclesiology threatens to eclipse church's existence as God's creature and to set church over against God's other creatures. It can suggest an essential asymmetry between church and world, a one-way relationship of dependence. Instead, a wisdom ecclesiology affirms church's creaturely interdependence with others. In its relationship with fellow creatures, church is both a giver and a receiver of gifts.

To claim church as the extension of the incarnation also risks reversing the flow of ecclesial dependence on Christ, as if the risen Christ were now absent and in need of an earthly stand-in. An ordinary-time ecclesiology declares that Christ is the divine life savingly translated into a creaturely medium, and it does not permit church to supplant Christ in this role. The living Christ remains the head of his body and its savior (Eph. 5:23). Church is a sinful creature; it continues to need the salvation it proclaims. Tim Gorringe asks: "Can anyone say without flinching or without horror that Christian activity in history has been in continuity with Jesus?"[24] Church's transparency to Christ is seen not least in its penitence. Its ministry of word and sacrament and mission is a proclamation of its ongoing dependence on Christ's grace and forgiveness.

The metaphor of church as the extension of the incarnation is especially dangerous when connected to a triumphalist Christology. According to this view, Christ's resurrection erases the tragic vulnerabilities and sufferings of Jesus's life and death. The risen Christ is raised above the contingencies and ambiguities of creaturely life, and it is this triumphant risen life that is mediated without remainder to the community of his followers. The stability and security of the earthly church, especially in its possession of sacred sacraments, creeds, and orders of ministry, becomes a visible confirmation of Christ's resurrection victory. Church becomes like the troublemakers in Corinth, claiming a wisdom and strength in Christ that bears no trace of the weakness and foolishness of the cross. "Already you have all you want! Already you have become rich!" (1 Cor. 4:8).

Triumphalist views of church are a betrayal of Christ's earthly life and a betrayal of the Christian call to follow his way of life on earth. In an ordinary-time ecclesiology, the metaphor of church as the extension of the

---

24. Timothy Gorringe, *A Theology of the Built Environment: Justice, Empowerment, Redemption* (Cambridge, UK: Cambridge University Press, 2002), 246.

incarnation is viable only in a very loose sense as church's ongoing embrace of the ambiguities and vulnerabilities of Jesus's earthly life. God's work of redemption takes time; it was not completed on the cross, nor at the resurrection. Through "the patient pedagogy of God's Spirit," it continues in the church's life. Church lives in the world as Jesus did, sharing its creaturely life. It accepts its dependence on others, the permeability of its boundaries with the world. The correspondence between church and the story of Jesus is multivalent and paradoxical, not direct and one to one. Church is Mary's child, "living without insulation" from the world's sorrows and failings.[25] Church is Mary, bearing Christ into the world through the power of the Holy Spirit. Church is a servant, ministering to Christ in every stranger (Matt. 25:34–40). Church is Peter, bitterly repenting its denials of its Lord. Church is the crippled woman whom Jesus sets free (Luke 13:10–13), joyfully witnessing to the inauguration of God's reign of liberation and justice. Guided and fed by Christ, accountable to his judgment, Christians are to be his disciples in the world, embracing the limits and joys of life in the flesh.

Christ's resurrection has indeed changed our humanity—and given us a new way to live in the world. This does not mean living above the fray of creaturely tensions and challenges, or pretending that God's work of sustaining and redeeming all that exists has now been funneled exclusively through the life of the church. But it does mean living with a nondefensive hopefulness about God's promised reign of creaturely communion and the part church has to play in this. Even in its imperfections and provisional nature, church trusts that its "life is hidden with Christ in God" (Col. 3:30). It does not have to be jealous of its social prerogatives or anxious to defend its moral and theological probity. Even its ordinary, modest acts of discipleship are validated and used by God. Being Christ's disciples is less a matter of claiming secure possessions than of being a centrifugal force of God's love in the world. The principalities and powers are still about their work of division and alienation, and church is not immune to their sway. But in Christ, through the Spirit, God fills the world with God's own imperishable life. Sorrowing, suffering, and alienation will not have the last word. In its finite, creaturely life, church lives to proclaim and embody this good news.

25. Nicholas Lash, *Theology for Pilgrims* (London: Darton, Longman and Todd, 2008), 30.

CHAPTER 5

Church as Earthen Vessel

I am debtor to all, to all am I bounden,
Fellowman and beast, season and solstice, darkness and light,
And life and death.

—Edwin Muir, "The Debtor"

A s the two preceding chapters argued, Christ is both the one in whom all things hold together and Mary's child. This dialectic between universal and particular carries over into the life of the community of Christ's followers. Church is a trustee of a radically universal vision of creaturely communion with God, impatient with the dividing walls of hostility (Eph. 2:14) that continue to alienate us from one another. At the same time, church, like Mary's child, is bound to an earthly identity and unable to escape material dependency. Church in ordinary time thus aims to be neither an island of heaven in the sea of earthly reality, nor the sacred legitimation of any existing worldly order. It sits at an angle to earthly arrangements, neither wholly transcending them nor wholly aligned with them. This chapter explores this ecclesial tension with the help of Paul's metaphor of "treasure in earthen vessels" (2 Cor. 4:7).

James Gustafson unpacks the double affirmation of this Pauline phrase: "The Church is *earthen* —of the stuff of natural and historical life. The Church is a *vessel*, it is useful."[1] Church is valued by God and useful pre-

---

1. James Gustafson, *Treasure in Earthen Vessels: The Church as a Human Community*, 3rd ed. (Louisville: Westminster John Knox, 2009), xviii.

cisely in its earthen character, not in spite of it. To call church an earthen vessel affirms its common creatureliness. It comes from the clay out of which the Creator shaped all things, fired in the kiln of the Holy Spirit to a fragile strength. In the wise foolishness of God, the precious treasure of the gospel is stored in clay jars.

No pastor has to be reminded that church is an earthen vessel. The chips and cracks of its creatureliness are in full evidence. Christian life is never primarily a theological recital of God's saving deeds, a matter of standing above the fray of daily experience and witnessing to the timeless truths of the gospel. Church conserves the treasure of the gospel through attention to the ordinary tasks of nurture and education, through concrete decisions about mission, as well as through worship and sacraments. Being a community whose daily life embodies the universal good news of the gospel is always a work in progress. The good that God intends for church has to be worked out in creaturely existence, and thus there is no way to avoid negotiation, error, risk, and change. In all its earthen ordinariness and particularity, church is by God's grace a provisional sign of something extraordinary and universal: God's promised restoration of all things (Acts 3:21).

"God has given Christ, the head of all things, to the church, which is his body, filled by the one who fills all things completely" (Eph. 1:22b–23). My account of church's identity as an earthen vessel is in accordance with this translation by Allen Verhey and Joseph Harvard in their commentary on Ephesians.[2] Church is filled by Christ, but it is not "the fullness of Christ" (a more typical English translation) in the sense that Christ's life is wholly absorbed by church and ceases to "fill all things completely." Christ is "the head of *all* things," not only the head of his body, the church. Church is not the glorious fullness itself but rather draws life from Christ and invites others to share in this life. Ecclesial life is derivative, dependent life. The emphasis is not on the splendor of the vessel but on the splendor of the treasure it holds—however clumsily.

All clay comes from the earth, but its properties vary by region, and so does the pottery that is made from it. Likewise, the earthen vessel of church

---

2. Allen Verhey and Joseph S. Harvard, *Ephesians*, Belief: A Theological Commentary on the Bible (Louisville: Westminster John Knox, 2011), 61.

varies from place to place, reflecting the influence of local climate and culture. The anonymous "Letter to Diognetus," written in the second century, gives a famous account of this natural variety:

> For Christians cannot be distinguished from the rest of the human race by country or language or customs. They do not live in cities of their own; they do not use a peculiar form of speech; they do not follow an eccentric manner of life. . . . Yet, although they live in Greek and barbarian cities alike, as each man's lot has been cast, and follow the customs of the country in clothing and food and other matters of daily living, at the same time they give proof of the remarkable and admittedly extraordinary constitution of their own commonwealth.[3]

Christianity has no permanent geographical center, no permanent official language. Church is a community of communities, each rooted in the land, language, and customs of its particular place. With the great swell of Christian communities of faith in the southern continents in recent decades, perhaps at no other time in Christian history has church looked as much like Revelation's vision of "a great multitude that no one could count, from every nation, from all tribes and peoples and languages" (Rev. 7:9). Christians have discovered the folly and harm that flow from pretending that cultural identities and human associations need to be erased or can simply be put aside to make room for the gospel. Conversion is a matter of *turning* the cultural forms already present to Christ. Thus there is no generic template for the earthen-vessel church: every expression of Christian faith embodies the distinctive *terroir* of its particular cultural location. The Christian commonwealth is formed by the sharing of irreducibly different voices and gifts. God works salvation through the specificity and concreteness of different cultures. Global Christian unity cannot be achieved by declaring the church in any particular time or configuration to be the full and final expression of church.

The earthen vessel of church varies from place to place, and in each place it bears similarities to the other earthen vessels around it. Church is

---

3. "Letter to Diognetus," in *Early Christian Fathers*, ed. and trans. Cyril C. Richardson (New York: Macmillan, 1970), 216-17.

always fashioned from the local cultural dust. As the "Letter to Diognetus" witnessed in its day, Christians do not live in self-referential, self-enclosed communities of language and practice. Bound by time and space as are other creatures, made of the same clay, they do not create a distinctive Christian world of meaning from scratch. In both a local and global sense, Christians live in a common world with others, sharing language, dress, and political arrangements. Christians are born into social settings they did not make or choose, settings that deeply and permanently mold them and their expressions of Christian faith. Pretending otherwise is a dangerous form of theological self-deception. Francine Cardman notes: "By denying that the church is like other human institutions, particularly political ones, ahistorical ecclesiologies mask the ways in which the church acts markedly like them."[4]

Among the ways church is distinguished from the other earthen vessels around it is by its self-relativizing insistence on an eschatological vision of universal creaturely communion with God. This means, as the "Letter to Diognetus" declares, that with cultural belonging also comes alienation. Christians "live in their own countries, but only as aliens. They have a share in everything as citizens, and endure everything as foreigners."[5] As an earthen vessel, church knows that being an earthen vessel is a provisional, improvisatory way of life. Christians in every place face the challenge of discerning how and to what extent existing identities and loyalties can be commended and nurtured in service to the universal vision of Christ's gospel. Not all earthly loyalties can be brought to serve that vision, and discerning those loyalties has never been easy. Sometimes Christians err on the side of disdaining the cultural "clay" of their earthly lives in an illusory attempt to free themselves from historical roots and material belonging. More often, though, Christians accommodate and assimilate too much to cultural and national identities.

Church has at times surrendered its universal vision of all things holding together in Christ and contented itself with being a clay pot conserving

4. Francine Cardman, "Myth, History, and the Beginnings of the Church," in *Governance, Accountability, and the Future of the Catholic Church*, ed. Francis Oakley and Bruce Russett (New York: Continuum, 2004), 33.

5. "Letter to Diognetus," 217.

only local cultural treasures. Thomas Merton gives a jaundiced description of the Church of England as a vessel of the English ruling class, whose treasure is

> a big, vague, sweet complex of subjective dispositions regarding the English countryside, old castles and cottages, games of cricket in the long summer afternoons, tea-parties on the Thames, croquet, roast-beef, pipe-smoking, the Christmas panto, *Punch* and the London *Times* and all those other things the mere thought of which produced a kind of a warm and inexpressible ache in the English heart.[6]

Merton would later discover that communal life in the Roman Catholic Church was also susceptible to an inappropriate enshrining of local customs and values. The larger point is that, while cultural belonging is intrinsic to creaturehood, all forms of cultural belonging are fallen and thus open to Christ's judgment: all deserve critical scrutiny, and some will have to be discarded as fundamentally alien to the universal vision of the gospel. Blood-and-soil religion in its many varieties is a constant temptation for Christian communities: it is all too easy to trim faith to fit inside the boundaries of our prior loyalties, to make faith in Christ a servant to familial and cultural and nationalist ends. This was Dietrich Bonhoeffer's painful recognition about the German elevation of the Aryan *Volkstum* as "the Archimedean point, that fixed, unquestionable point of departure," to which the Christian message was asked to justify itself.[7] Allegiance to the Christ who fills all things disrupts these cozy alliances, demanding an allegiance to the whole earth and to all peoples. The apostle Paul's insistence that our citizenship is in heaven (Phil. 3:20) should be understood in this vein. Our heavenly citizenship does not mean that ordinary political dynamics are not operative in church, much less that church has the perfect political template that everyone else needs to live by. Christians are not removed from particular earthly allegiances altogether (as if that were even possible),

6. Thomas Merton, *The Seven-Storey Mountain* (New York: Harcourt, Brace and Co., 1948), 66.

7. Dietrich Bonhoeffer, *Theological Education at Finkenwalde: 1935–1937*, Dietrich Bonhoeffer Works, vol. 14 (Minneapolis: Fortress, 2013), 414.

but they pledge a loyalty to Christ that challenges the narrow boundaries of these allegiances.

In this light, we must also scrutinize allegiance to the earthen vessel of church. Even more than bonds of family and nation, the earthly church makes a legitimate claim on us—though this, too, is a penultimate claim. Our ultimate citizenship as Christians is found in heaven, not in church. Allegiance to church should not trump allegiance in Christ's name to the whole earth and to all peoples. Simone Weil declares that "imperfection comes from attaching yourself to the Church as to an earthly country.... The children of God should not have any other country here below but the universe itself, with the totality of all the reasoning creatures it ever has contained, contains, or ever will contain. This is the native city to which we owe our love."[8] With earthly ecclesial belonging also comes alienation. Church is called by God to be an earthen vessel that *knows* it is an earthen vessel, spurning absolutist visions for its own finite, vulnerable life.

The problem is that this self-relativizing vision of church fits all too well with the role assigned to church by modern, liberal nation-states. All religious communities are equally disestablished in this regime: they must remain penultimate, so that ultimate human loyalties can be claimed by the state. For a wisdom ecclesiology, the point of spurning absolutist visions of church is of course not to make room for absolutist visions of the state! Instead, it is a reminder of the provisional, fallen character of all human institutions. Yet the state has sought to usurp this absolutist role time and time again in the modern period. Practical Christian wisdom is needed here to nurture practices, social forms, and ways of thinking and living in the world that can keep Christians and others from ceding ultimate loyalty to the state. An ordinary-time ecclesiology welcomes a healthy religious pluralism that fosters the active and discriminating participation of various mediating communities in the affairs of the larger society. This respectful cooperation with religious others is undergirded for Christians by the insistence that all persons share the same core identity as beloved creatures of God. Along these lines, Rowan Williams has distinguished between an appropriate "procedural secularism," which refuses to give advantage or preference to any one religious community over others, and an inappropriate "programmatic

---

8. Simone Weil, *Waiting for God* (New York: Harper and Row, 1973), 96–97.

secularism," which seeks to rid the public space of all particular religious allegiances.[9] Christians should embrace the former, seeking to join hands with members of other religious communities to address the issues that concern our common creaturehood in all its social and ecological ramifications.

Principalities and Powers

Earthen vessels take up space, and space is never a neutral theological category. This means that questions of the built environment, which "provides us with all the most direct, frequent and unavoidable images and experiences of everyday life,"[10] are relevant to a wisdom ecclesiology. Individual and corporate human agency has material effects: the human world as we encounter it is physically shaped by social ideals and practices. These ideals and practices become sedimented in architectural forms, building codes, and zoning laws. The built environment both embodies conscious decisions about human community and shapes how communal life in those spaces is experienced. Church is no exception to this.

Walter Wink's famous example of a "dead church" shows that ecclesial configurations of the built environment can send a message that contradicts or even silences the spoken liturgy: "What could the priest say that could counteract the thunderous statement made by a building erected on the site of a razed Inca temple, by virtual slave labor, adorned with gold leaf stolen from a high civilization by a group of Spanish thugs, and whose chapel had been converted into a curio shop?"[11] Church neighborhood locations, parking lots, and seating plans preach their own sermons. Before a single liturgical word is uttered, they make a theological statement about the kind of community church is—who is invited and who is excluded, what is valued and what is insignificant. The social-material flesh of Christian communities is shaped by space as well as by story and sacrament.

9. Rowan Williams, *Faith in the Public Square* (London: Bloomsbury, 2012), 2–3.

10. Maf Smith, John Whitelegg, and Nick J. Williams, *Greening the Built Environment* (London: Earthscan Publications, 1998), 13; see also Timothy Gorringe, *A Theology of the Built Environment: Justice, Empowerment, Redemption* (Cambridge, UK: Cambridge University Press, 2002).

11. Walter Wink, *Unmasking the Powers* (Philadelphia: Fortress, 1986), 74.

Christian life is an intrinsically communal life, and all earthly communal life needs forms of organization. Structures and the institutions they inhabit are necessary means of creating and sustaining connections among people, and hence of creating communal identity. Like architecture, dress, and language, organizational structures reflect the local cultural clay. They are part of the earthen character of church and will vary from place to place. An account of church in ordinary time neither disdains nor absolutizes institutional structures. Every Christian community has polity (that is, political) decisions to make about ordering its common life. Communities of faith need ways of organizing and distributing power in order to produce a way of life that is both sustainable and transparent to their convictions about God and God's purposes. This includes God's purposes for creaturely life: as an earthen vessel, church is not free to disregard the exigencies and dependence of embodied creaturehood.

Like patterns of cultural belonging and use of space, earthly ways of ordering church life are part of the creaturely "thrones or dominions or rulers or powers" (Col. 1:16) that are created through Christ and are in need of Christ's redemption. They are both indispensable and fallen. An ordinary-time ecclesiology has no refuge in a privatized or abstract conception of Christian faith that pretends that structures and institutions are irrelevant to true Christian identity and have no theological significance. On the other hand, this ecclesiology refuses to idealize existing ecclesial structures, recognizing that they do not pass through earthly power arrangements like water through a pipe but are shaped by the complexities and accidents of human history. Christians have always thought about church order with the moral and political tools their culture gives them.

The struggle over appropriate ways of ordering Christian community is apparent from New Testament times onward. The earliest Christians' conceptions of church reflected in different ways the assumptions of a patriarchal society with an agrarian base and a household-centered, slave-supported, urban apex.[12] Their appropriations of this social vision for Christian communal life exhibit both accommodation and resistance. Across the centuries,

---

12. This description is from Wayne A. Meeks, "The 'Haustafeln' and American Slavery: A Hermeneutical Challenge," in *Theology and Ethics in Paul and His Interpreters*, ed. Eugene H. Lovering Jr. and Jerry L. Sumney (Nashville: Abingdon, 1996), 232–53.

Christians have appropriated and adapted various models of human organization that were available in the larger society: the household, the empire, the nation-state, and the corporation, to name a few. None of these models has been wholly successful in conserving the treasure of the gospel, and each of them has implications for how Christian communities relate to the larger social order. Like all forms of human society, church is caught up in the contingencies of historical conditionedness.

The political and creedal shape of particular Christian traditions reflects the confluence of various theological, historical, and cultural factors. Evolving social visions and cultural circumstances have encouraged modifications of existing polity structures and the development of new ones. For example, lay leadership was a predominant feature of Chinese Catholic communities—long before the Second Vatican Council's renewed emphasis on the laity—because of its affinity with patterns of folk-Buddhism.[13] Pentecostal forms of leadership have flourished in the developing capitalist societies of Latin America in the contemporary period, both as cultural protest and cultural accommodation.[14] The formation and defense of church polity never occur in a political or cultural vacuum. The enormous diachronic and synchronic breadth of church life and witness serves as a hedge against perennial tendencies to absolutize particular historical contexts and the polities appropriate to them.

Differences in polity generally prove more intransigent than doctrinal differences in ecumenical relations, a reminder of how deeply faith is nurtured and shaped by material structures. As Ola Tjørhom has argued, it is not productive to hold up a particular Christian polity as the standard against which to measure the ecclesial density of others.[15] Polity for an earthen-vessel church is a practical matter, guided by theological and pastoral concerns. The

13. Richard P. Madsen, "Catholicism as Chinese Folk Religion," in *China and Christianity: Burdened Past, Hopeful Future*, ed. Stephen Uhalley Jr. and Xiaoxin Wu (Armonk, NY: M. E. Sharpe, 2001), 233–49.

14. Andrew Walker, "Thoroughly Modern: Sociological Reflections on the Charismatic Movement from the End of the Twentieth Century," in *Charismatic Christianity: Sociological Perspectives*, ed. Stephen Hunt, Malcolm Hamilton, and Tony Walter (New York: Palgrave Macmillan, 1997), 17–42.

15. Ola Tjørhom, *Visible Church—Visible Unity* (Collegeville, MN: Liturgical Press, 2004).

emphasis is on function and usefulness. Thus a wisdom ecclesiology commends the contribution of the historic episcopate to the unity and stability of the church across the centuries and in the present; yet it concurs with the assertion of the ecumenical document *Baptism, Eucharist and Ministry*:

> [I]t is increasingly recognized that a continuity in apostolic faith, worship, and mission has been preserved in churches which have not retained the form of historic episcopate. This recognition finds additional support in the fact that the reality and function of Episcopal ministry have been preserved in many of these churches, with or without the title "bishop."[16]

On the other hand, a wisdom ecclesiology acknowledges that the divisiveness of denominational Protestantism has wounded church life and mission and been a key contributor to the accelerated religious fragmentation that has characterized the modern West. Particular ways of ordering Christian communal life are worthy of theological reflection, but they are not themselves the treasure of the gospel. They are provisional, they are never perfect, and they are always means to a greater end.

Roman Catholic, Orthodox, Anglican, and various Protestant forms of church government have all been vigorously defended on the basis of Scripture, history, theology, and the pragmatics of church life. But as the Christian center of gravity moves southward, it seems increasingly clear that the terms of the debate among these broad traditions are bound up with the religious and cultural history of Christendom: that is, they do not shed much light on the increasingly wide swaths of church that do not fall into any of these confessional categories. In an account of church in ordinary time, the ecumenical question is not which one, if any, of these classical polities is normative in and of itself, but how there is to be global communion, that is, a common possession of material and spiritual riches among the world's Christians. A wisdom ecclesiology presses even beyond this, wanting church "to imagine community for the sake of the wider human community, and wider human community for the sake of the earth which sustains us."[17]

---

16. *Baptism, Eucharist and Ministry*, Faith and Order Paper no. 111 (Geneva: World Council of Churches, 1982), para. 37.

17. Gorringe, *Built Environment*, 249.

From Constantine to Henry VIII to Vladimir I, shifts in church polity have been inseparable from global politics. Various kinds of "ruler-friendly" polities have been developed over the centuries, and access to large amounts of political and social power has been a factor in some of church's most shameful moments. When Christians have forgotten what the "Letter to Diognetus" calls the "extraordinary constitution of their own commonwealth," they have tried to achieve ecclesial security through alliances with political power and to coerce others into belonging. The challenge for an earthen vessel church is to use the cultural resources available to give a nondefensive witness to Jesus Christ that sits at an angle to the current configurations of this world, including the current configurations of church. Christians are to order their communal lives to display both their hopes for God's promised future and their roots in God's earth. The goal of all ecclesial arrangements is to weave together ways of life in union with Christ—for the sake of the whole world. This will require both the cultivation of distinctively Christian practices and joining hands with non-Christians to pursue common social goods.

Sacraments

Contemporary Christian piety has popularized the Celtic metaphor of "thin places." This metaphor trades on the notion that material reality is a barrier to the presence of God: a veil separates the spiritual and material realms. Yet this veil is not of uniform thickness, and there are places where it thins to the point of becoming, in George MacLeod's words, "only tissue paper."[18] Places of quiet and scenic beauty, those furthest from the routines of ordinary life, are favorite candidates for thin places. And the desire for thin places is understandable. Carving out space for prayer and contemplation within the scrum of daily life is vital for faith. Christians need regular ways of ordering their bodily lives to pay attention to God's presence, and quiet and beauty can help. However, a wisdom ecclesiology rejects the theological assumptions implicit in a spiritual attachment to thin places: God is not mostly absent from the world, accessible only in special thin places. God is the creator of

18. Ron Ferguson, *George MacLeod: Founder of the Iona Community* (Glasgow: Wild Goose Publications, 2001), 156.

everything, free to meet us in all times and places. Material reality is God's gift, not a barrier to God's presence. All our experiences of God come to us as embodied creatures. Therefore, when we think about sacraments, giving an account of church in ordinary time turns the metaphor of thin places on its head. It celebrates sacraments as "thick places," places where the physical concreteness of our daily lives and God's presence and promises link up most clearly.[19]

Jesus Christ is the primordial sacrament, the invisible God becoming ordinary visible flesh in Mary through the power of the Spirit. In the incarnation, creaturely senses are the primary receptors of God's truth and presence. This privileged role for the senses continues in the sacraments of baptism and Eucharist, as rooted in Christ's own practice and evolved over the centuries in the communities of his followers.[20] God's presence in the sacraments is never separated from God's activity, and we should thus resist the theological temptation to posit static manifestations of divine power in the elements themselves or in the clergy presiding over them. By the power of the Spirit, these sacraments "incorporate" us into Christ's body and nourish the ongoing life of that body. Christian fellowship is a shared participation in the blood and body of Christ (1 Cor. 10:16–17).

Beyond the official sacraments recognized in different Christian traditions, other things that church does are sacramental in a derivative sense, since whenever "two or three are gathered together," Christ promises to be in their midst (Matt. 18:20). The Second Vatican Council's *Lumen Gentium* promulgated the metaphor of church *as* sacrament: a sign and instrument of union with God and of the unity of all humankind. As with the metaphor of church as a continuation of the incarnation, caution is in order. As Avery Dulles notes, there is considerable ambiguity "about what the Church as sacrament or sign represents. Is the church, as we commonly experience

---

19. This is perhaps closer to another of George MacLeod's famous sayings: that God is to be found and praised in the midst of creaturely life—"in the High St."—rather than tucked away in a sanctuary.

20. This section focuses on baptism and Eucharist, which are the sacraments with the widest ecumenical recognition. However, the exact number of official sacraments is not of great concern to a wisdom ecclesiology, and I suspect that my general sacramental approach can be extended for Christian traditions with a more expansive understanding of sacraments.

it, a convincing sign of the unity, love, and peace, for which we hope in the final kingdom?" Dulles concludes that the pilgrim church is not such a sign, "even in a provisional manner."[21] In church's ongoing struggle to embody unity, love, and peace, it points to humanity's ongoing need for the grace Christ bestows.

To call church a sacrament is not to imply that the world outside its boundaries is bereft of Christ's grace. The Spirit is like a wind that blows where it wills, and the presence of the risen Christ is not restricted to ecclesial contexts. Even an encounter with a needy stranger can be a place to meet Jesus (Matt. 25:40).[22] Since in Christ all things hold together, creaturely reality outside church can also be a material means of connection with Christ. Though no part of creaturely reality is beyond the reach of Christ's presence and agency, baptism and Eucharist are privileged as outward and ordinary means of being united with Christ. Christ is truly and transformingly present in these sacraments, present via the power of the Spirit in ordinary earthly things like water, wine, and bread, and in the communal actions surrounding those materials. The physical elements and communal actions of the sacraments are not an impediment to divine presence; they are the medium of divine presence. In them, Christians are communally formed and transformed in ways that surpass their own agency. Baptism and Eucharist are thick places where God meets us in the glory of ordinary creaturely life.

Earthly Elements

Sacraments have often been treated as thin places, consigned to rarified religious realms that are far removed from the problems and joys of everyday life. Their celebrations occur within the precincts of clerical power, often behind what Martin Luther King Jr. called "the anesthetizing security of stained glass windows."[23] Thus understood, a theology of the sacraments

21. Avery Dulles, *A Church to Believe In* (New York: Crossroad, 1985), 5.

22. The presence of Christ is what defines a sacrament. I am thus resisting proposals in various creation-oriented theologies to posit the cosmos as the primary sacrament, so that the sacramentality of Jesus is derived from the sacramentality of the cosmos (see, e.g., Dorothy C. McDougall, *The Cosmos as the Primary Sacrament* [New York: Peter Lang, 2003]).

23. Martin Luther King Jr., "Letter from a Birmingham Jail," in *A Testament of Hope: The*

might seem to have little to learn from the biblical Wisdom literature, which shows very little interest in religious ritual and concerns itself instead with life before God in the ordinary settings of home, fields, and marketplace. Bringing biblical wisdom to bear on sacramental reflection is a reminder that our sacramental life is indeed connected to the concerns of those ordinary settings. Sacraments are thick with questions about agriculture and economics, with concerns about the flourishing of communal and creaturely life. The water of baptism flows into concerns for how water resources are shared and protected. The Eucharistic table connects to other tables in human life—kitchen tables and boardroom tables—raising questions about how to distribute power and resources so that all are fed. Sacraments link up with other forms of divine blessing in that they concern "the addressing and claiming of earthly life for God."[24] Bonhoeffer warns Christians against adopting "the customary, overspiritualized" approach to blessing that pretends to supersede God's earthly blessings.[25] "The cup of blessing" (1 Cor. 10:16), like other forms of divine blessing, is bound up with our lives as needy, dependent creatures. An ordinary-time ecclesiology insists on keeping the connections between sacraments and ordinary life strong.

Sacramental celebrations are a distillation of the whole of Christian life: they involve communal gathering, receiving, sharing, testifying, and being sent into the world. From a wisdom perspective, the focus of sacraments is less on the authority of the celebrant or the special properties of the elements than on the way of life they invite believers into. As David Willis notes, in the Eucharist the Holy Spirit makes use of "ordinary bread and wine, their breaking and pouring and chewing and swallowing, to be instruments of Christ's presence and consequently of renewed repentance, forgiveness, and walking in newness of life."[26] In both baptism and Eucharist, the Holy Spirit uses ordinary, earthly elements to unite ordinary, earthly creatures to Christ. God gives both creaturely life and new life in the Spirit through what is impermanent and changing. Like the creatures who receive them, the

---

Essential Writings and Speeches of Martin Luther King, Jr., ed. James M. Washington (San Francisco: HarperSanFrancisco, 1991), 299.

24. Dietrich Bonhoeffer, *Letters and Papers from Prison*, Dietrich Bonhoeffer Works, vol. 8 (Minneapolis: Fortress, 2010), 492.

25. Bonhoeffer, *Letters and Papers from Prison*, 492.

26. David Willis, *Notes on the Holiness of God* (Grand Rapids: Eerdmans, 2002), 93.

sacramental elements are temporary, transient. They must be received when they are given: they evaporate and mold and ferment.[27] Within the circular rhythms of the earthly biome, the sacramental elements are constantly being transformed. Water from rainfall becomes grapes; bread digested becomes human flesh. In a kind of reverse transubstantiation, the earthly substance of God's creation remains constant in all the sacramental elements, while the accidents differ. Sacraments are creaturely gifts for the creaturely people of God. They are a central part of the Holy Spirit's bodily curriculum.

"If we were incorporeal," declares Calvin, echoing John Chrysostom, God would have bound us to himself in "naked and incorporeal" ways. Since "we are creatures who always creep on the ground" and "cleave to the flesh," God graciously uses material means.[28] Yet Protestants, in particular, have often seemed to long for incorporeality. According to a favorite image of the Protestant Reformation from Romans 10:14-17, church is a creature of the Word (*creatura verbi*). This is often understood in terms of the word of Scripture, highlighting the centrality of the Bible and its proclamation for church life. Christian faith in "logocentric" theologies is primarily about hearing and knowing the good news of Jesus Christ's redemption of sinful humanity. In fact, Protestant theology often seems to imagine human beings as creatures possessing enormous ears to hear the word, with all their other sense organs left to atrophy. Hearing is the place where the thick veil separating the spiritual and material worlds thins. The preferred creaturely medium for the Spirit is assumed to be the invisible airwaves, not visible water and bread.

Gathering around the texts of Scripture is central to the rhythms of life lived in God's presence, and I will explore that in the next chapter. However, a lopsided emphasis on the scriptural word has resulted in a sacramental anemia in some Protestant traditions. Sometimes sacraments are accorded secondary status as "visible words," an aid to the hearing impaired. On one

27. Serene Jones, "Setting the Table: Meanings of Communion," in *Setting the Table: Women in Theological Conversation*, ed. Rita Nakashima Brock, Claudia Camp, and Serene Jones (St. Louis: Chalice Press, 1995), 264. See also Leanne Van Dyk, "The Gifts of God for the People of God: Christian Feminism and Sacramental Theology," in *Feminist and Womanist Essays in Reformed Dogmatics*, ed. Amy Plantinga Pauw and Serene Jones (Louisville: Westminster John Knox, 2006), 204-20.

28. John Calvin, *Institutes of the Christian Religion* 4.14.3, ed. John T. McNeill, trans. Ford Lewis Battles (Philadelphia: Westminster, 1960), p. 1278.

hand, this is a recognition of how the promises of God in Scripture are brought home for us as embodied creatures when they take tangible form. It is often not until water is splashed and bread is broken that our eyes are opened (Luke 24:31). Calvin says that "sacraments bring the clearest promises."[29] On the other hand, a cognitive grasp of the gospel message is still given such priority in the sacramental scheme of "visible words" that children, those with cognitive disabilities, and others who have difficulty understanding the preached word are often discouraged from coming to the table or, in believer-baptism traditions, from being baptized in the first place.

A wisdom ecclesiology insists on a more central role for sacraments in church life than some Protestant traditions have allowed. When connection to God comes predominantly by hearing, Christians have little opportunity to "taste and see that the LORD is good" (Ps. 34:8). Church is not only a creature of the spoken and heard word of Scripture; it is a creature of the Word in whom all things hold together, the Word made flesh in Mary's child. Since church is a creature of the Word who embraced both the joys and the neediness of creaturely life, it is appropriate that church is also a creature of water, wine, bread, and oil. Earthly followers of Jesus Christ need the word of the gospel, but they also need to be washed, fed, healed, and anointed. Sacraments attend to and echo basic creaturely needs and delights. They make clear that union with Christ is not only about forgiveness of sins and personal inward change. It is also an affirmation and intensification of the original grace of creaturely life. Sacraments meet us where we are, as creatures who live in utter dependence on God's material provisions, whose physical senses are the vehicles for spiritual transformation. We need physical signs of Christ's presence—both as sinners and simply as creatures. We are God's dependent and needy creatures before we are agents of witness to the gospel of Jesus Christ. Sacramental celebrations are communal occasions to give thanks for God's gift of creaturely life and to receive gifts needed to sustain it and redeem it. Communion with Christ and each other happens through our bodies.

Baptismal and communion liturgies are often clearer about the links between sacraments and creation than are formal theologies of the sacraments, which tend to stay within the theological orbit of human sin and redemption.

---

29. Calvin, *Institutes* 4.14.5, p. 1280.

The liturgies link the water of baptism to the waters of creation and the flood. They link the bread and wine of the Eucharist to the bounty of fields and vineyards. Prayers of thanksgiving in sacramental celebrations are for both God's creative and redemptive blessing. God creates water and the fruit of the earth, and uses them again and again both to sustain our creaturely lives and to re-create and save us. An ordinary-time ecclesiology insists that we do not lose this larger purview in more formal theological reflections on the sacraments. God's grace in the sacraments is not divorced from the original grace of creation. Even apart from sin, human creatures need water and nourishment as well as ongoing reminders that they are not their own makers and keepers. As often as we witness a baptism or taste communion wine, we remember and receive God's grace in our creaturely lives. God's gracious provision for creaturely needs is part of what sacraments respond to and celebrate.

Gordon Lathrop notes that baptism both locates and liberates.[30] Baptism locates us: we are not baptized with water in general, but with the water of a particular place. Baptism roots us in a local geography, in the physical life of a local community of believers. It also links us to all the creatures who share a dependence on that local source of water, which means that concerns about the ecological condition of watersheds are baptismal concerns. We receive God's gifts and live out our faith from a particular creaturely location. Yet Lathrop insists that baptism is also liberating—moving us beyond any settled parochialism. The local water of our baptism is connected to water everywhere. The local community into which we are baptized is part of the global body of Christ, for whom there is "one Lord, one faith, one baptism" (Eph. 4:5). Baptism creates a solidarity with people and places far beyond our local horizons. On a larger scale, baptism is also liberative in resisting confinement to anthropocentric ways of ordering the world. Lathrop warns us against a cosmology that puts our watery planet at the center of everything. In Christ, *all* things hold together, including the incalculable expanse of waterless places in our universe. In baptism we claim our humble place as thirsty, earth-bound creatures of God: we stand "at the edge of this precious,

<hr />

30. Gordon W. Lathrop, *Holy Ground: A Liturgical Cosmology* (Minneapolis: Fortress, 2003). The treatment of baptism in this paragraph is indebted to Lathrop's discussion, 97–124, esp. 105.

life-generating water," and give thanks.[31] The bread and cup of the Eucharist also come from the life-giving water of the earth, and they embody a local *terroir*. They, too, locate us in a specific time and place and yet put us in solidarity with Christ's disciples of every earthly time and place, united by the power of the Spirit and also by our creaturely needs.

Sacraments Gone Wrong

Sacraments affirm our common creaturehood, even though they have sometimes been used to deny it. Sacraments sometimes function less as a means of grace than as a marker of spiritual superiority, separating the faithful from those who are thought to lack the prerequisite faith and holiness. When this happens, church denies the ongoing creaturely need that stands behind the sacraments. The title character in Marilynne Robinson's novel *Lila* goes to the river to try to wash off her brand-new baptism after she overhears her pastor husband and his friend calmly discussing the fate of the unbaptized. Lila realizes that none of the people who had loved and cared for her in her earlier life had been baptized, and the idea that her baptism confers a grace that somehow separates her from them fills her with revulsion. If sacramental grace separates her from Doll, Mellie, Doane, and Marcelle, she wants no part of it. In her hunger for solidarity with those who are "strangers to the covenants of promise" (Eph. 2:12), Lila reclaims the grace-filled logic of baptism. In heaven, she concludes, "it must always be true that there are the stragglers, people somebody couldn't bear to be without, no matter what they'd been up to in this life."[32] Baptism is a sign for all stragglers of the breadth of Christ's grace. It binds Christians both to each other and to all those in physical and spiritual need.

As Lila's story shows, sacramental symbols of incorporation and nurture can become instruments of human exclusion and alienation. Like all other aspects of church life, sacraments are subject to abuse. Our desperate need for sustenance and redemption can be manipulated and perverted. The apostle Paul insists that "we have this treasure in clay jars, so that it may be

---

31. Lathrop, *Holy Ground*, 105.
32. Marilynne Robinson, *Lila: A Novel* (New York: Farrar, Straus and Giroux, 2014), 258.

made clear that this extraordinary power belongs to God and does not come from us" (2 Cor. 4:7). Church has sometimes forgotten this. Sacraments can tempt clergy to claim for themselves divine power with which to dispense or withhold grace. Sacramental elements can become idols. Sacramental celebrations can be used to reinforce racial and economic divisions. Church lives in the paradox of affirming God's good sacramental gifts while acknowledging the sinful misuse of them. Church needs to exercise practical wisdom in assessing its sacramental practices without giving in to the temptation to flee or despise the bodily curriculum of the Spirit.

On one hand, the power of sacraments is not dependent on human holiness. Christians trust that God is graciously at work in the midst of human sin. In the original grace of creation, God continues to lavish sunlight and rain on both the just and the unjust (Matt. 5:45). By the same token, God is at work in the midst of—and even in spite of—sinful church practices. Sacramental grace is given despite and in the midst of corrupt priests and unworthy recipients. Calvin observes that what "God has ordained remains firm and keeps its own nature, however people may vary."[33] The lavishness of God's grace shines especially brightly through the cracks of human brokenness. On the other hand, a wisdom ecclesiology cannot afford any indifference to how sacraments function in ordinary time. The horrific ways in which the sacraments have at times been celebrated deserve to be repudiated; they also deserve to be incorporated into sacramental reflection. Our theologies of baptismal grace should not ignore the forced baptism of Moriscos in sixteenth-century Spain. Our Eucharistic theologies should take into account the role deliberate racial segregation at the communion table played in the legitimation of apartheid in twentieth-century South Africa. Sacramental theology has often been content to revel in normative visions or exemplary case studies. An account of church in ordinary time is oriented toward the concrete and is thus attentive to the gaps between normative accounts of how sacraments "should be" and the much messier reality of how they actually function in particular contexts.[34] A wisdom

33. Calvin, *Institutes* 4.14.16, p. 1291.
34. An excellent theological account of such a gap is found in Mary McClintock Fulkerson and Marcia W. Mount Shoop, *A Body Broken, a Body Betrayed: Race, Memory, and Eucharist in White-Dominant Churches* (Eugene, OR: Cascade Books, 2015).

ecclesiology calls church to "keep the feast," while refusing to ignore the sacramental abuse of God's gifts.

The apostle Paul displays this wisdom orientation in his concern for the way the Lord's Supper was being celebrated in first-century Corinth. In 1 Corinthians 11, he chastises rich Christians for eating the bread and drinking the cup in ways that humiliated their poorer brothers and sisters. Sacraments aim at union in love with both God and neighbor. They are given as a means of divine grace and of mutual human edification: Christians receive these divine gifts only as they join with others. Sacraments have both vertical and horizontal dimensions, and Paul accuses the Corinthians of failing to keep the horizontal dimension in view. In their celebrations of the Supper, the Corinthians were "showing contempt for the church of God" (1 Cor. 11:22). They were eating and drinking without "discerning the body" (1 Cor. 11:29). God's blessings of both creaturely life and sacramental grace continue to flow. But God calls us to receive these blessings in ways that are attentive to creaturely and communal flourishing. Rather than using God's gifts to build up and edify, we can use them in counterproductive ways that break down and alienate the social body. Paul charges the Corinthians with eating the bread and drinking the cup "in an unworthy manner" (1 Cor. 11:27): when rich Christians humiliate their poor brothers and sisters, they are celebrating the Supper in a way that sabotages community and alienates them from God's purposes for creaturely flourishing and mutual edification. God's blessings continue to flow, but they become a form of judgment.

According to Paul, a result of the Corinthians' selfish and divisive celebrations of the Lord's Supper is that some have become "weak and ill, and some have died" (1 Cor. 11:31). Within Paul's wisdom orientation, this should not be understood as a divine punishment extrinsic to human choices and actions. Bodies—both individual bodies and corporate bodies—get sick when human creatures fail to practice solidarity and discernment. They eventually weaken and die. As Woman Wisdom declares, "those who miss me injure themselves; all who hate me love death" (Prov. 8:36). In making us new creatures in Christ (2 Cor. 5:17), the Spirit does not despise the interdependent patterns of our original creation. No member of Christ's body can say to another, "I have no need of you" (1 Cor. 12:21). Sacramental practice is not insulated from creaturely requirements for communal flourishing. Nor should we regard health and long life as a divine reward given *in exchange* for appropriate "discernment of the body" in sacramental celebrations. Rather, we should, with Howard Thurman, "see the finger of God moving in the natural unfolding of antecedents and consequences."[35] The grace God intends in the sacraments is woven into the patterns of our communal flourishing as God's creatures, and in the shaping of these patterns, the needs of the most vulnerable deserve priority.

Sacraments as Foretaste

The sacraments are an experience of both intimacy and absence. They celebrate the gracious nearness of Christ's presence in our midst, while at the same time they plead, "Come, Lord Jesus" (Rev. 22:20). By the power of the Spirit, the sacramental elements are a vehicle for grace, but they do not circumscribe Christ's presence in the material world. Christ is truly present in the community of his followers, but he does not become their possession. The risen Christ is not confined to the earthen vessel of church and its practices, because he continues to be the head of all things, filling them completely (Eph. 1:22b–23).[36] The sacraments both incarnate and intensify a longing for God that is never fully realized on earth. The pouring of baptismal water signals our desire for a full immersion in God's life. Sharing the Eucharistic elements nurtures our hunger to be fed at God's eschatological banquet table. Our earthly experience of God's grace, whether communicated by biblical word, by sacrament, or in some other way, is never absolute or final.

The tensive quality of our experience of sacramental union also extends to the horizontal dimension of the sacraments. Recognition of each other's baptisms and Eucharistic sharing both presuppose ecclesial unity and are a means to further Christian unity. Unity for an earthen-vessel church is

---

35. Howard Thurman, "What Shall I Do with My Life?" in *Callings: Twenty Centuries of Christian Wisdom on Vocation*, ed. William C. Placher (Grand Rapids: Eerdmans, 2005), 387.

36. In this way, a wisdom ecclesiology resonates with the Christological principle known as the *extra calvinisticum*. Though its name links it to Reformed concerns about the idolatry of circumscribing the divine within creaturely truths and goods, this principle has roots back to the early centuries of Christian reflection. See, e.g., Athanasius, *On the Incarnation* 17: "The marvelous truth is, that being the Word, so far from being Himself contained by anything, He actually contained all things Himself."

always a work in progress, leaving room for the abundant richness of diverse forms of historical creaturely life. Earthly sacramental celebrations will always be linked to the water, the soil, and the culture of particular places. In addition to this earthly diversity, sacramental celebrations have never been entirely free from social and theological divisions. From the Last Supper onwards, there has never been full unity among Christ's disciples— nor a fully common sacramental understanding. This acknowledgment of perennial sacramental dissension is not a reason for complacency in today's church: the divided Eucharist remains "a bleeding wound in the ecumenical movement."[37]

An account of church in ordinary time celebrates the unity already present among Christians in their common devotion to Jesus Christ—and yearns for more. Within the bodily curriculum of the Spirit, Christian love and unity are strengthened and nurtured by the thickness of shared sacramental practice. Sacraments do not simply signal unity already achieved: they are embodied means to deepening Christian unity. Recognition of each other's baptisms leads to an impatience with the dividing walls that prevent us from living out our shared commitment to Jesus Christ. Eucharistic sharing creates a holy hunger for the fullness of communal life in Christ. Perfect union in love with God and each other remains an eschatological gift yet to be realized. On the way to that promised future, as Margaret Farley notes, "even imperfect unity and imperfect love can help us to cast out fear."[38]

The unity that Christians desire is ultimately bigger than church: it is the unity of the whole creation in God's reign of peace. Sacraments are a foretaste of that perfect union, celebrated in hope of and for the sake of that great unity. Sacraments locate us in the present, uniting us in our shared needs and hungers, but they also point beyond themselves. A wisdom ecclesiology refuses to identify church's earthly forms of life with the final realization of God's purposes for creation. Sacramental celebrations both affirm the original grace of creaturely life and lean into God's promised future: they are what church does until Christ comes (1 Cor. 11:26).

37. Kondothra M. George, "Editorial," *The Ecumenical Review* 44 (January 1992): 1.
38. Margaret A. Farley, "No One Goes Away Hungry from the Table of the Lord," in *Practice What You Preach: Virtues, Ethics, and Power in the Lives of Pastoral Ministers and Their Congregations*, ed. James F. Keenan and Joseph Kotva Jr. (Franklin, WI: Sheed and Ward, 1999), 198.

PART 3

Church in the Power of the Spirit

Following the Trinitarian structure of this book as a whole, this third part explores church in the power of the Holy Spirit. The Nicene Creed calls the Holy Spirit "the Giver of Life," and this title reflects the peculiar double-edgedness of Christian traditions concerning the Spirit. The Spirit has always had an institutional affiliation: the one who indwells the followers of Christ, binding them together in love and giving them new life. But there has always been another side: the mysterious and free Spirit who "blows where it chooses" (John 3:8), transcending church structures and even the boundaries of human society to renew the whole creation. This universal edge of the Spirit's work cuts against church's perennial attempts to cage the Spirit, restricting its role to granting a seal of divine approval to established ecclesial patterns and teachings. New life in the Spirit is nurtured and practiced in church, but it is not confined to church. A wisdom ecclesiology explores the ecclesial work of the Spirit without losing sight of its universal dimensions.[1] It rejects accounts of the Spirit that attempt to distance church from other forms of creaturely life, either by emphasizing the immediacy or immateriality of the Spirit's work, or by setting church radically apart from all other communities. Dietrich Bonhoeffer says, "Jesus calls not to a new religion but to life."[2]

The work of the Spirit is oriented toward God's promised future, and

---

1. I explore these themes further in "The Holy Spirit and Scripture," in *The Lord and Giver of Life: Perspectives on Constructive Pneumatology*, ed. David H. Jensen (Louisville: Westminster John Knox, 2008), 25–39.

2. Dietrich Bonhoeffer, *Letters and Papers from Prison*, Dietrich Bonhoeffer Works, vol. 8 (Minneapolis: Fortress, 2010), 482.

this teleological bent keeps church from becoming either complacent or despairing about the incompleteness and failures of its communal life. Yet it is a theological mistake to ignore the cyclical dimensions of the Spirit's work. The bodily pedagogy of the Spirit accommodates the constraints of our temporal creaturehood. The Spirit's movement from old to new, from death to life, takes time—both for individuals and for communities. It takes repetition and practice. The story of Jesus's coming, suffering, death, and resurrection needs to be told and lived out again and again. The Spirit does not disdain the commonplaces of church life, the recurring rhythms of prayer, worship, nurture, and mission.

The work of the Spirit is punctuated by surprising acts of power, reminding church that its future is not confined by what seems possible in the present. Yet it is a theological mistake to view ordinary church life as "a struggle across dull plateaus between peaks of spiritual refreshing."[3] A wisdom ecclesiology affirms the power of the Spirit in the places and processes of ordinary time, and not only in extraordinary signs and wonders. The new life given by the Spirit is new *creaturely* life, not some exalted spiritual life that leaves creaturehood behind. As Bonhoeffer notes in his doctoral dissertation, *Sanctorum Communio*, "it is precisely in the context of everyday life that church is believed and experienced. The reality of church is understood not in moments of spiritual exaltation but within the routine and pains of daily life—and within the context of ordinary worship."[4] The Spirit calls church to both lean forward and dig deep, to announce and embody its future hope and to live in grateful acknowledgment of its creaturely grounding in God's original grace.

The chapters of part 3 emphasize the cyclical and ongoing dimensions of the Spirit's work by tracing the arc of the Christian liturgical year. In response to the movement of the Spirit, church lives its life in different registers. These registers are postures of faith that respond to the gospel of Christ in the concreteness of creaturely life. They are less a set of discrete activities or practices than communal orientations of the heart. They are more about the

---

3. Sidney E. Mead, *The Lively Experiment: The Shaping of Christianity in America* (New York: Harper and Row, 1963), 125.

4. Dietrich Bonhoeffer, *Sanctorum Communio: A Theological Study of the Sociology of the Church*, Dietrich Bonhoeffer Works, vol. 1 (Minneapolis: Fortress, 2009), 281.

"how" than the "what" of Christian existence. The mystery of Christian faith embraces what Bonhoeffer called "the polyphony of the whole of life."[5] Life in the Spirit is not about *either* sorrow *or* joy, *either* Lent *or* Easter, but all of them together at the same time. Yet this polyphony is too much for temporal creatures to learn all at once. It helps to pull some of the melodies of this life apart and pay attention to them one at a time—in a repetitive cycle. In the lives of both individuals and local communities these registers are not confined to a particular liturgical season, and they observe no predictable order. Longing is not confined to Advent, for example, and it is not always the case that after a night of weeping, "joy comes with the morning" (Ps. 30:5). Yet rehearsing the different melodies and living into the different modalities of faith throughout the church year gives Christians a repertoire to draw on in everyday life. Communities of Christians who regularly read the Psalms know this well. By participating in the ongoing rhythms of the community of saints, Christians learn how to weep and how to laugh, and also *when* to weep and *when* to laugh (Eccles. 3:4).

Chapter 6 focuses on the liturgical season of ordinary time, where church spends most of its days. The special creaturely significance accorded to ordinary time throughout this book also permeates the treatment of the other seasons of the church year in the chapters that follow: Advent (chap. 7), Christmas (chap. 8), Lent (chap. 9), Easter (chap. 10), and Pentecost (chap. 11). The Holy Spirit blows through each of these liturgical seasons—over and over again. The corresponding registers of Christian life in the Spirit are indicated by the gerunds of the chapter titles: "Making New and Making Do" (ordinary time), "Longing" (Advent), "Giving" (Christmas), "Suffering" (Lent), "Rejoicing" (Easter), and "Joining Hands" (Pentecost). These gerunds also indicate that becoming attuned to the rhythms of life lived in God's presence is an ongoing process. It takes time.

---

5. Bonhoeffer, *Letters and Papers from Prison*, 397. I explore this image further in the epilogue.

CHAPTER 6

Making New and Making Do

> When the song of the angels is stilled,
> When the star in the sky is gone, . . .
> The work of Christmas begins.

—HOWARD THURMAN, "The Work of Christmas"

The ordinal ("counted") weeks of ordinary time that occur in the spaces between the celebrations of Advent, Christmas, Lent, Easter, and Pentecost make up most of the church year. A wisdom ecclesiology aims to give a theological account of the importance of this ordinary time. Of course, in the wake of Christ's resurrection, no time is really ordinary time. Church lives in the gap between the resurrection and the last things. God's reign has been inaugurated but is not yet here in fullness. We carry in our bodies both the death of Jesus and the life of Jesus (2 Cor. 4:10). Karl Barth calls this time between the first coming of Christ and his awaited second coming "the time of the community."[6] This time is a gift given in God's providence, an opportunity for the community's service and witness to Christ. For an ordinary-time ecclesiology, this includes cultivating the practical wisdom that conduces toward the flourishing of human life and the whole creation.

Like all creaturely time, "the time of the community" is of uncertain and

---

6. Karl Barth, *Church Dogmatics*, IV/1, ed. G. W. Bromiley and T. F. Torrance, trans. G. W. Bromiley (New York: T&T Clark, 1956, 2004), 725.

finite duration. There is no temple in the new Jerusalem (Rev. 21:22). When the new Jerusalem comes, the work of the earthly church will be done. To shift to Paul's eschatological metaphor, church waits and longs for the time when God will be all in all (1 Cor. 15:28). Ordinary time is in-between time: since Christians do not know the day or the hour of God's promised consummation of all things, they are called to live faithfully within the opportunities and constraints of the present. Providence, as Joe R. Jones notes, is "a grammar of a long and meaningful middle."[7] "Give us this day our daily bread" (Matt. 6:11) is church's prayer as it lives in the long and meaningful middle of ordinary time.

Because Christ has already been raised, new life in Christ's Spirit begins now—in ordinary time—while God's creation is still groaning for deliverance from its bondage to decay (Rom. 8:21–22). The rhythms of the life-giving Spirit echo the rhythms of creation: in the midst of old and dying life, new life gradually appears. Yet Christian understandings of the Spirit's work have often betrayed a preference for the immediate, the dramatic, and the linear, as if the authentic mark of the Spirit's power were the circumvention of ordinary temporal and creaturely limits. Rachel Muers points out that this circumvention of creaturely finitude in order to secure immediate success is how the Gospel accounts portray Christ's temptations by Satan. The power of the Holy Spirit, Muers insists, "works precisely with and within [our] temporal and creaturely limits."[8] There are seasons of Easter in church life, times of surprising newness that call forth jubilant celebration. But most of church time is ordinary time, in which the Spirit's work of sanctification is a gradual disciplining of the full range of our creaturely capacities and desires for responding faithfully to God. By word and sacrament, prayer and mission, the Spirit patiently teaches us new ways to live as creatures in God's world, wiser ways of loving God and neighbor. Church in ordinary time aims to be a lifelong school of the Spirit, where, in Augustine's words, "we learn something every day."[9]

7. Joe R. Jones, *A Grammar of Christian Faith: Systematic Explorations in Christian Life and Doctrine*, 2 vols. (Lanham, MD: Rowman and Littlefield, 2002), 1:259.

8. Rachel Muers, "The Holy Spirit, the Voice of Nature and Environmental Prophecy," *Scottish Journal of Theology* 67, no. 3 (2014): 339.

9. Augustine, "Sermon 16A," in *The Works of Saint Augustine: A Translation for the 21st Century*, vol. 3/1: *Sermons 1–19* (Brooklyn, NY: New City Press, 1990), 347.

Some Christians, especially certain varieties of Protestants, have resisted the bodily curriculum of the Spirit, lured by the illusion of a disembodied spirituality unencumbered by the limits and demands of material life. With Huldrych Zwingli, they have affirmed that "the Spirit needs neither guidance nor vehicle for he is himself the power and the means by which everything is carried."[10] According to this account, the Spirit spurns material means, and those who live in the Spirit should likewise aspire to a faith that transcends their material existence. This view of the Spirit relies on a disastrous conflation of two senses of *flesh* in the New Testament: the Word made flesh in Jesus Christ (John 1:14) and the sinful way of the flesh, which is opposed to the Spirit (Gal. 5:17). In ecclesiology, this bifurcation of spiritual and material reality has contributed to the sacramental anemia that I criticized in the preceding chapter. It has encouraged understanding the Spirit's work primarily in individual terms, a matter of bringing people to experience personal renewal and embrace true teachings, leading them to make a conscious choice to follow Jesus. This, in turn, has shaped approaches to worship and evangelism that seem to deny that our fleshliness is a proper locus for our life of faith.

An ordinary-time ecclesiology rejects this bifurcation between spirit and body—and between intellect and emotion—as illusory and dangerous. The Spirit's way of bringing new life accords with the kind of communal creatures we are: the kind who learn through our bodies and are drawn through our loves. We are analyzing and interpreting beings in and through our capacities as sensing and feeling beings. Our identities as individuals are formed in community. The Spirit's sanctifying work concerns whole persons, whole communities—indeed, the whole creation. The work of the Spirit is transgressive, pushing embodied human creatures toward each other across cultural and racial divides, so that different material ways of life become joined and quilted together. Eugene Rogers declares: "The Spirit is a Person with an affinity for material things."[11] Life in the Spirit means sharing this affinity, affirming our creaturely identities and our creaturely place in the world God loves.

10. Gottfried W. Locher, *Zwingli's Thought: New Perspectives* (Leiden: Brill, 1981), 217.

11. Eugene F. Rogers, *After the Spirit: A Constructive Pneumatology from Sources outside the Modern West* (Grand Rapids: Eerdmans, 2005), 60.

Practices

A wisdom ecclesiology's emphasis on church as a place of lifelong embodied learning fits well with recent interest in Christian practices.[12] The concept of practice highlights the importance of communal bodily wisdom in grounding theological knowledge and sustaining Christian traditions. While some theological approaches to practices have argued for the radical incommensurability of Christian practices with those of other communities, an account of church in ordinary time insists that the doctrine of creation remain on the theological horizon. God's original grace situates us in a creaturely ecology, and it is there that the Spirit is at work.

Our lives are not self-contained, either biologically or culturally. Embodied life is a shared life: we borrow ourselves from others.[13] As Maurice Merleau-Ponty observes, to be a body is "to be tied to a certain world."[14] Through our bodies we are tied to other creaturely bodies, to what we perceive through our senses, and to the material resources we depend on in everyday life. Through our bodies we are also perceived and judged by others, and that, too, forms and deforms our identity: how we are habitually *seen* shapes who we are. Our bodies tie us to centuries of human attitudes and practices sedimented in patterns of land use, architecture, racial schemas, and political systems. This complex social history is "given body, *made body*"[15] in our communal lives. We are dynamic and malleable creatures, always being shaped by others, both for good and for ill.

Over time, we acquire what Pierre Bourdieu calls "systems of durable

12. For a helpful account of recent approaches and emphases, see Ted A. Smith, "Theories of Practice," in *The Wiley Blackwell Companion to Practical Theology*, ed. Bonnie J. Miller-McLemore (Oxford: Blackwell, 2012), 244–54.

13. Paraphrase of Maurice Merleau-Ponty, "Philosopher and His Shadow," in *Signs*, trans. Richard C. McCleary (Evanston, IL: Northwestern University Press, 1964), 159. I am indebted to Mayra Rivera's interpretation of Merleau-Ponty in *Poetics of the Flesh* (Durham, NC: Duke University Press, 2015). I agree with her that Merleau-Ponty does not adequately take into account the force of social constructions for how we encounter the world. As Rivera notes, sometimes what we "borrow" from others is our own negation (70).

14. Maurice Merleau-Ponty, *Phenomenology of Perception* (New York: Routledge, 1962), 171.

15. Pierre Bourdieu, *Outline of a Theory of Practice*, trans. Richard Nice (Cambridge, UK: Cambridge University Press, 1977), 94.

transposable dispositions,"[16] largely unconscious habitual ways of being in the world. This ordinary "know-how" for navigating the world resides in our bodies. Our bodily habituations to the particular configurations of the world around us forge our assumptions about what is normal and natural long before we consciously articulate them. But these habituations also make possible our personal agency, becoming the basis for what Bourdieu calls "regulated improvisation"[17] Our cultural malleability is key to the work of shaping and sustaining communal traditions, including religious traditions. As Mary McClintock Fulkerson notes, "the continuity of practices and, thus, of a tradition, requires enculturated bodily habituation with its learned everyday wisdoms and their entailed competence for ever-changing situations."[18]

The Spirit's work of sanctification is a transformation of our shared, embodied life, and thus of our "enculturated bodily habituation"—with its "learned everyday wisdoms." This transformation happens in ordinary time, as the Spirit sets us on a communal journey from solidarity in sin to a solidarity in wise holiness. This journey is not a denial of our creaturely dependencies and vulnerabilities. It does not erase our bodily ways of knowing and navigating the world. Nor does it detach us from our identities as culturally and historically situated creatures. Sanctification involves "the redemption of our bodies" (Rom. 8:23), as we discern and rehearse together the moves and reflexes that put us in step with Christ.

As we saw in the preceding chapter, there is no starting from scratch. The earthen vessel of church is fashioned from the local cultural dust, including its cultural toxicities. Christians are bound by time and place like other creatures, unable to transplant themselves into an utterly new social location of their own choosing. The cultural systems that we inherit and are habituated into are complex and morally ambivalent. We require "wisdom from above" (James 3:17) to discern what in us and in our wider culture must be renounced, and what can be lived with and adapted to.[19] This selection

16. Bourdieu, *Outline of a Theory of Practice*, 72.

17. Bourdieu, *Outline of a Theory of Practice*, 79.

18. Mary McClintock Fulkerson, *Places of Redemption: Theology for a Worldly Church* (Oxford: Oxford University Press, 2007), 47.

19. H. Richard Niebuhr's landmark *Christ and Culture* is helpful in showing different Christian styles of relationship with culture; unfortunately, it tends to treat culture as a uniform phenomenon.

and reconstruction of cultural materials is not a once-for-all, all-or-nothing kind of operation. Discernment about cultural renunciations and transformations is an ongoing and imperfect process both because of the variability of the cultures in which church exists and because church, like other forms of creaturely life, is always conflicted and in flux. Therefore, life in the power of the Spirit is a matter of "making new and making do."

From the very beginnings of Christian faith, "making new" has never been a cultural creation ex nihilo.[20] Restorationist wistfulness about some "golden age" of Christian identity and purity is misplaced. Wayne Meeks insists that exaggerated claims for the uniqueness of the earliest Christian communities do not survive historical scrutiny: "Whatever was distinctive about the Christian movement was embodied in the diverse repertoire of social idioms shared in the larger culture."[21] Christians in every era have pursued their desire for holiness and freedom in Christ within the real confines of a given social world. In shaping their practices, Christians learn and borrow from others, using the cultural materials at hand to forge a way of life. Kathryn Tanner puts it this way: "Christian practices are always the practices of others made odd. . . . A Christian way of life is, then, essentially parasitic; it has to establish relations with other ways of life, it has to take from them, in order to be one itself."[22] Ordinary human practices like washing, eating, and giving witness are made new, born again in service to Jesus Christ. This process of making new is provisional and ad hoc, because the story of church is still unfolding, still unfinished. Living in the shadow cast already by the resurrection, church is able by the power of the Spirit to repent of old sins and risk new patterns of communal life.

These "born again" practices do not stay within some private Christian enclave: they share in the centrifugal force of the Spirit, reaching out beyond the porous boundaries of church. Christian practices such as healing, testimony, and forgiveness address fundamental human needs as well as the demands of religious formation; they are performed for the sake of the world, as well as for the edification of Christian communities of faith.[23] The new

20. See this recognition in the Vatican II encyclical *Gaudium et Spes*, para. 44.
21. Wayne A. Meeks, "The Irony of Grace," in *Shaping a Theological Mind: Theological Context and Methodology*, ed. Darren C. Marks (Burlington, VT: Ashgate, 2002), 53.
22. Kathryn Tanner, *Theories of Culture* (Minneapolis: Fortress, 1997), 113.
23. Craig Dykstra and Dorothy C. Bass, "Times of Yearning, Practices of Faith," in *Prac-*

life in the Spirit nurtured and practiced in Christian communities of faith keeps our common world in view. It does not run away from the problems of life in a pluralistic society and on a planet under ecological threat. Christian practices aim at embodied wisdom for a way of life that lives in gratitude to God and is aligned with God's purposes for all creation.

In the in-between time of church, "making new" exists alongside "making do." As Karl Barth insists, Christian life is a matter of "doing the relatively better relatively well."[24] Communal Christian practices are never perfect or pure; nor do they have to be in order to be habitations of the Spirit. Even though "we do not know how to pray as we ought" (Rom. 8:26), the Spirit intercedes for us. Marked by communal confusions and failings, Christian practices are not merit badges, evidence of the exemplary form of our communal life: they are like holding out our hands to receive the bread of life at communion; they are a communal act of faith that is at the same time a concrete acknowledgment that we are not whole, that we are not at peace, that we need healing and nourishment only God can provide. Making do is also an acknowledgment of creaturely limits—limits of time, energy, knowledge, and control over the creaturely forces around us. Even new life in the Spirit contends with these constraints. As Paul counsels the Romans, "If it is possible, so far as it depends on you, live peaceably with all" (Rom. 12:8). The Spirit's work is not a shortcut in the management of creaturely reality. New life in the Spirit accords with the kind of creatures we are.

The Wisdom books of the Bible are the biblical paradigm for making do. In the book of Proverbs, this awareness is articulated most clearly in the "better/than" proverbs: "Better is a little with the fear of the LORD than great treasure and trouble with it" (15:16). Often creaturely wisdom presents itself not in sharp contrasts, but in tradeoffs between competing goods. Growth in wisdom requires a patience that acknowledges creaturely limits and temptations. This growth also requires humility about our moral limits. Creaturely wisdom is inaccessible to those "who are pure in their own eyes" (Prov.

ticing Our Faith, 2nd ed., ed. Dorothy C. Bass (San Francisco: John Wiley and Sons, 2010), 1–12. My participation in the collaborative work on Christian practices by the Valparaiso Project on the Education and Formation of People in Faith helped spur my interest in developing a wisdom ecclesiology.

24. Karl Barth, *Church Dogmatics*, IV/4: *The Christian Life: Lecture Fragments* (Grand Rapids: Eerdmans, 1981), 271.

30:12). The book of Ecclesiastes emphasizes our need to make choices in the face of an unknowable future beyond our control. "Whoever observes the wind will not sow; and whoever regards the clouds will not reap" (Eccles. 11:4). Ecclesiastes also recognizes the fragility of goodness in a fallen world: amidst the wise and righteous efforts of many, "one bungler destroys much good" (Eccles. 9:18). The Wisdom books advocate a kind of holy resignation to the limits of our creaturely wisdom and power. While they are not in themselves a sufficient guide for a community living into the promise of the new creation in Christ (2 Cor. 5:17), they are useful in guarding Christians from both fantasy and resentment regarding their creaturely limits. New life in the Spirit does not sweep away uncertainty, frustration, and the need for compromise.

A winsome example of making new and making do is found in George Herbert's *The Country Parson*. The country parson, Herbert notes, "is a lover of old customs, if they be good and harmless." Even when parts of these old customs have become rotten, "he pares the apple, and gives them the clean to feed on."[25] As an example, Herbert lifts up the benefits of communal procession. The practice of processing around the geographical boundaries of the parish has a long history, probably dating back to pre-Christian Britain. While the focus was at one time on "beating the bounds" to drive out evil spirits, Herbert affirms the practice's evolution to emphasize four things: gratitude for God's blessings on the fruits of the field; justice in preserving communal property boundaries; opportunities for love and reconciliation among the participants; and generosity toward the poor.[26] Here is an old custom made new, and used by the Spirit to cultivate communal gratitude, justice, reconciliation, and generosity. Yet the wise parson is alert to the ambiguity of communal practices and how easily a practice "passeth from good to bad."[27] He is not naïve about the stubborn presence of human sin and misery, through which God is "dishonored every day, and man afflicted." Rather than descend into bitterness and "perpetual severity," the parson exhibits wise and sometimes even cheerful resignation. He "condescends

25. George Herbert, "The Country Parson," in *The Country Parson, The Temple*, ed. John N. Wall Jr., The Classics of Western Spirituality (New York: Paulist Press, 1981), 109.

26. Herbert, *The Country Parson*, 109.

27. Herbert, *The Country Parson*, 92.

to human frailties both in himself and others," and "intermingles some mirth in his discourses."[28] God's unshakeable love for creatures and for sinners, not the purity of church practices, is the root of Christian identity and assurance.

The bodily curriculum of the Spirit often proceeds at a slower pace than we would like, and making do with our constraints and failings as God's finite creatures has proved difficult for Christians, particularly when it comes to understandings of church. As Bonhoeffer notes, we often love our dream of Christian community more than Christian community itself.[29] We are tempted to romanticize some past era in church life, or to hitch ourselves to an idealized version of what church should be. This temptation is especially pronounced in the "turn to the ecclesial subject" that puts church at the center of Christian dogmatics.[30] Ted Smith observes that guiding most methodological turns toward culture in contemporary Christian theology and ethics is "the logic of *Gemeinschaft*." This logic posits a normative Christian culture, "entirely different from our own culture, marked by wholeness and coherence, and supercharged with clear religious significance: other, whole, and ideal."[31] Whether the unifying theme is mission, communion, liberation, or something else, Christians long for a consistency and wholeness in church practices, a clear communal purpose and identity that will set church apart from the messy, conflictual chaos of the world.

While an account of church in ordinary time understands the lure of this logic of *Gemeinschaft*, it insists instead on the humble, self-relativizing logic of making new and making do. Our ordinary communal life is clear evidence that the extraordinary power of the gospel "belongs to God and does not come from us" (2 Cor. 4:7). Church does not pretend to have already realized the full hope of the Spirit in its own life, nor to have the capacity to bring this hope to fruition by its own actions. Some ecclesial hopes for purity and uniqueness will never be realized. Some of those hopes must, in fact, be

28. Herbert, *The Country Parson*, 95.

29. Dietrich Bonhoeffer, *Life Together*, Dietrich Bonhoeffer Works, vol. 5 (Minneapolis: Fortress, 1996), 36.

30. I use this phrase in chap. 1 above to describe a particular contemporary approach to ecclesiology.

31. Ted A. Smith, *The New Measures: A Theological History of Democratic Practice* (Cambridge, UK: Cambridge University Press, 2007), 23.

deliberately relinquished to better accord with the boundary-crossing ways of the Spirit. "It does not yet appear what we shall be" (1 John 3:2 RSV).

Scripture

Scripture, like sacraments, is a central part of the Spirit's bodily curriculum and a primary instance of the cyclical nature of the Spirit's work. The Spirit draws us into the future by making us an embodied community of memory. Christians have lived with the same texts of Scripture century after century. Through these old words, the majority of them written neither by Christians nor for Christians, the Spirit continues to bring new life. Christian sanctification never progresses to the point of being able to set the letter aside. Calvin frequently reminded his Genevan listeners that "we are not more virtuous or more excellent than our fathers," and so we stand in need of the same assurances of God's forgiveness and mercy.[32] The canon of Scripture, in its different ecumenical variations, binds communities of Christian faith to a particular set of texts, and to each other as common readers and hearers of those texts. Scripture has a unique, privileged place in church life as an anchor of communal identity. Yet, as was the case with sacraments, a wisdom ecclesiology's approach to Scripture attends more to the new way of life guided by these texts than to their special properties.

The Bible is for Christians the most important form of what Paul Connerton has called "inscribed memory," what a community writes down and passes on from generation to generation. Our discussion of practices has already highlighted the significance of what Connerton calls "incorporative memory," a communal "knowledge and a remembering in the hands and in the body."[33] Both are needed. The diachronic identity of church is lodged in and transmitted through the words of Scripture and through the practices of our bodies. In fact, these two kinds of communal memory blur together when it comes to the practice of Scripture. Orienting ourselves to Scripture's

32. John Calvin, commentary on Isaiah 48:13, in *Commentary on the Book of the Prophet Isaiah*, vol. 4, trans. William Pringle (Edinburgh: Calvin Translation Society, 1853), 44.

33. Paul Connerton, *How Societies Remember* (Cambridge, UK: Cambridge University Press, 1989), 95.

demands and promises always involves our bodies. Discerning "what the text means" entails, in Wayne Meeks's words, "the competence to act, to use, to embody, and this capacity is also realized only in some particular social setting."[34] Both the context and the aim of reading Scripture are fundamentally tied up with embodied practice. The words of Scripture "receive their setting and their meaning only in physical participation in the worship [and life] of a Christian community."[35] Discerning the Spirit when reading Scripture is inseparable from modes of social performance.

Like other practices of Christian life, Scripture, too, is a matter of making new and making do. The Spirit works through the particular writings of Scripture, with all their disturbing angularities and baffling silences. In recognizing the authority of precisely this canon of voices, Christians confess that these writings are "*sufficient* for the ends to which they ought to be used in the church."[36] The promise of the Spirit is neither that Scripture has been infallibly written nor that it will be infallibly read, but that these writings are sufficient to nurture and shape our love toward God and neighbor. There is not one set of proper reading practices. Every generation, in every social context, has to discover the power of Scripture anew. Womanist readers of Scripture find new hope and strength for resisting oppression in the story of Hagar in Genesis. Chinese Christians, steeped in a cultural reverence for ancestors, find comfort and guidance in Paul's reflections on meat offered to idols in 1 Corinthians 8. Church "makes do" with the texts of Scripture it has received from the hands of others, and in the process it finds that, through the illuminating work of the Spirit, those texts are continually made new. Their meaning and power for our communal lives is never exhausted.

The Bible has often been the last bastion in attempts to preserve the "logic of *Gemeinschaft*" with respect to Christian practices. Here, some would claim, we have a whole, consistent, ideal source for Christian iden-

---

34. Wayne Meeks, "A Hermeneutics of Social Embodiment," *Harvard Theological Review* 79 (1986): 184. I explore the embodied practice of reading Scripture further in "The Lay Practice of Scripture," in *Sharper Than a Two-Edged Sword: Preaching, Teaching, and Living the Bible*, ed. Michael Root and James J. Buckley (Grand Rapids: Eerdmans, 2008), 63–81.

35. Margaret R. Miles, *Bodies in Society: Essays on Christianity in Contemporary Culture* (Eugene, OR: Cascade, 2008), 12.

36. David H. Kelsey, *The Uses of Scripture in Recent Theology* (Minneapolis: Fortress, 1975), 105 (italics in original).

tity. Some would maintain that, while Christians are borrowers and scavengers when it comes to shaping communal practices, this dependence on others does not go all the way down because it is normed by the Bible. We ascribe to the Bible—or, more accurately, Christians' imaginative construal of a story inscribed there—an originary autonomy that keeps the Christian use of borrowed materials "on a distinctively Christian track."[37] A wisdom ecclesiology declares that the pattern of "making new and making do" extends even to the contents of Scripture. We have already seen this in the intellectual ecumenism of the Wisdom literature in general, and Proverbs's direct literary dependence on *Instruction of Amenemope* in particular.[38] In the New Testament, the household codes are an example of making new and making do with existing Greco-Roman social norms. Christians are indeed called to live in the world Scripture creates, but this is an interdependent and cross-cultural world. There is no insulated, self-contained source for Christian life in the Spirit.

Luke 24 tells the story of Jesus's interpretation of Scripture to two disciples on the way to Emmaus: "Beginning with Moses and all the prophets, he interpreted to them the things about himself in all the scripture" (Luke 24:27). Yet, as the disciples later report this encounter to the others, they say that Jesus was "made known to them in the breaking of the bread" (Luke 24:35). As David Ford reflects on this, "the main point of [Jesus's] teaching about himself is not contained in the teaching: that just opens the way for the recognition and vanishing in the breaking of bread." Ford sees here a wise recognition of the limits of wisdom—"even when it is taught by Jesus—and a fortiori about the limits of textually-conveyed wisdom."[39]

Scripture remains church's indispensable witness during this time between the times. All the other registers of church life explored in the following chapters receive their orientation from the communal reading of Scripture. Like the sacraments, Scripture is a provisional treasure, gratefully practiced until Christ comes.

---

37. Kathryn Tanner describes and critiques this approach in *Theories of Culture*, 114.

38. See the introduction.

39. David Ford, "Jesus Christ, the Wisdom of God," in *Reading Texts, Seeking Wisdom: Scripture and Theology*, ed. David F. Ford and Graham Stanton (Grand Rapids: Eerdmans, 2004), 13.

CHAPTER 7

Longing

What we will be has not yet been revealed.

—1 John 3:2

The church year begins in longing. The liturgical cycle starts with the season of Advent, a season of waiting for the coming of Christ into the world. Though church's existence is predicated on the fact that Christ *has* come, many parts of God's world seem bereft of Christ's healing and transforming presence. Church also longs for the fullness of Christ's presence in its midst, mending all that is broken and bringing the joy of salvation to its promised fruition. Because Christ has indeed come, most of the seasons of the liturgical year are a response to the Word made flesh and dwelling among us: year after year, church celebrates Christ's birth, death, and resurrection, and the pouring out of Christ's Spirit on all flesh at Pentecost. But these celebrations do not erase the keen sense of Christ's absence. "O Come, O Come, Immanuel," Christians continue to pray. Longing for God is a permanent feature of church life on earth.

Out of this longing for God flows longing for a communal way of life that reflects God's power and presence. The sixth-century theologian Thalassios the Libyan declares that Christians are drawn together by their common longing: "An all-embracing and intense longing for God binds those who experience it both to God and to one another."[1] Church longs to live as a vis-

---

1. Thalassios the Libyan, *The Philokalia*, vol. 2 (London: Faber and Faber, 1981), 307.

ible community of those who have received God's mercy in Christ and have been brought "out of darkness into his marvelous light" (1 Pet. 2:9–10). This identity is both a gift and a calling, and the gap between them yawns wide. Leonardo Boff observes: "We profess: Christ delivered us from sin! And we keep on sinning. He delivered us from death! And we keep on dying. He reconciled us with God! And we keep on making ourselves God's enemies."[2] An ordinary-time ecclesiology refuses the consolation of ascribing finality to some dimension of the life, practices, or structures of church. Christians are bound together in their longing, not in their secure spiritual and institutional achievements. In their longing to live fully into their baptismal identity as "heirs of God and joint heirs with Christ" (Rom. 8:17), Christians join with the sighs of the Holy Spirit, hoping for what they do not yet see (Rom. 8:25–26).

Church longs for what lies beyond earthly life and beyond history, for the day when "mourning and crying and pain shall be no more" (Rev. 21:4). But that does not translate into an indifference to earthly flourishing here and now. Bonhoeffer says: "Only when one longs for life and the earth so much that with it everything seems to be lost and at its end may one long for the resurrection of the dead and a new world."[3] Within the framework of a wisdom ecclesiology, it is appropriate for church to "long for life and the earth," and in this longing church joins its voice with the voices of the Wisdom books. Longing in the Bible is usually associated with the Psalms and the prophets, but longing is common to all who trust in God. The biblical Wisdom books voice this longing for earthly flourishing in distinctive registers. The insistent expressions in Proverbs of the triumph of wisdom, life, and righteousness over folly, death, and wickedness are, as Roland Murphy rightly notes, "more a matter of trust and hope than of experience."[4] In Ecclesiastes, the teacher Qohelet voices radical skepticism about grand human designs to transcend the vulnerability and finitude of creaturely life by grasping for power or glory, or by hoarding treasure for oneself. In a world

2. Leonardo Boff, *Passion of Christ, Passion of the World* (Maryknoll, NY: Orbis, 2001), 86.

3. Dietrich Bonhoeffer, *Letters and Papers from Prison*, Dietrich Bonhoeffer Works, vol. 8 (Minneapolis: Fortress, 2010), 213.

4. Roland E. Murphy, "Wisdom and Creation," in *Wisdom and Psalms*, ed. Athalya Brenner and Carole Fontaine (Sheffield, UK: Sheffield Academic Press, 1998), 38.

in which calamity can fall without warning (Eccles. 9:12), human longing for earthly flourishing takes the form of small, concrete acts of solidarity. Job's exasperated responses to his friends and his anguished and angry questioning of God are expressions of longing for a world that makes moral sense, in which God's wisdom is manifest to human understanding. Whether trusting, skeptical, or anguished, all these voices belong in church. Church joins the "eager longing" of all creation (Rom. 8:21) for deliverance from poverty, violence, sickness, oppression, and everything else that thwarts creaturely flourishing. Our longing does not indicate the Spirit's absence: because the Spirit groans for the redemption of all creation, when we long for this redemption, we find ourselves joined even more closely to the Spirit—and by the power of the Spirit to all creation.

The Four Ecclesial Marks

The Nicene Creed professes "one, holy, catholic, and apostolic church." These four classical marks are marks of longing. It is evident that the four marks are not an empirical description of church, whose life has often mirrored the divisions, confusions, and failings of the larger society. The Christian calling to be one has been frustrated by church conflict and schism. Church's holiness has been persistently marred by sin. Its catholicity has been fragmented by bigotry and parochialism. Christian apostolicity has been compromised by insular self-satisfaction and a refusal to repent and learn from the wisdom of others. In keeping with its emphasis on the derivative, dependent character of church, a wisdom ecclesiology insists that the four ecclesial marks refer, first of all, to Christ. They refer to church only in union with Christ.

Church longs to be in conformity with the perfections of Christ. In him the four marks radiate outward with coruscating brightness, and in its worship and mission, church tries to stand close enough to Christ to reflect a bit of his glory. Jürgen Moltmann declares that the "acknowledgment of the 'one, holy, catholic and apostolic church' is acknowledgment of the uniting, sanctifying, comprehensive, and commissioning lordship of Christ."[5] The

---

5. Jürgen Moltmann, *The Church in the Power of the Spirit* (New York: Harper and Row, 1977), 338.

uniting work of Christ, gathering all his members into one body, is the basis for church's oneness. Membership is based on Christ's invitation alone, relativizing the rules and assumptions of ecclesial structures. The sanctifying work of Christ—justifying and bringing new life in the Spirit to sinners—is the basis for church's holiness. This is a *forgiven* holiness, not a pristine, perfected holiness. According to John Calvin, church is holy "in the sense that it is daily advancing and is not yet perfect."[6] The comprehensive presence of the risen Christ is the basis for church's catholicity. Just as no human boundaries can contain the life of the risen Christ, so church is sent by the Spirit to be a community without boundaries, a community in which all human cultures, races, and ways of life find a home. Willie Jennings notes that "the church should be the place that suspends the worry of how multiple peoples may coinhere together not by avoiding such complexity but through showing a collective body moving, living, and struggling to form a space of life and love."[7] Church is also catholic as it moves beyond its own fellowship through open-handed service to the whole created world, especially its suffering and vulnerable members. In its catholicity, church rejects all boundaries for its life that fall short of the human race. The commissioning work of Christ has been the basis for church's apostolicity from the beginning. Church is apostolic as its teaching and practice model faithfulness to the gospel of Jesus Christ across time. Apostolicity is not restricted to ordained leadership, nor to official ministries of word and sacrament. Church is called to be apostolic in its ordinary daily life, testifying to and enacting the apostolic teaching of Christ's love for the whole world. Apostolicity is less about preserving an unchanging substance than about carrying forward a living faithfulness to Christ. In all these ways church longs to live a life in Christ worthy of its calling (Eph. 4:1).

Church's longing to be one, holy, catholic, and apostolic is not simply for its own sake. The transformation of its life is always a means of participating in God's larger purposes for creaturely flourishing. Church's longing for God's will to be done on earth as in heaven translates into a profound

---

6. John Calvin, *Institutes of the Christian Religion* 4.1.17, ed. John T. McNeill, trans. Ford Lewis Battles (Philadelphia: Westminster, 1960), p. 1031.

7. Willie James Jennings, *Acts*, Belief: A Theological Commentary on the Bible (Louisville: Westminster John Knox, 2017), 157.

creaturely solidarity. This solidarity with other creatures is not passive or immobile. Janet Soskice insists that Christian hope "is angry for a better world," and here is where the otherwise problematic metaphor of "the church militant" gets some traction.[8] Church is militant in its refusal to stop longing and working for the creaturely flourishing of all. Church longs to be so filled with Christ's Spirit that its life in this world gives life to others. It cultivates a pragmatic wisdom about how it can contribute to a better world, without letting go of its apocalyptic hope in a God who can do more than it can ever imagine. Church nurtures its longing to sit at God's eschatological welcome table by feeding the hungry and outcasts. It intensifies its longing for the day when death will be no more (Rev. 21:4) by being present with the dying.

Adolescence and Maturity

In a daring analogy, Calvin declares that "the life of believers, longing constantly for their appointed state, is like adolescence."[9] Adolescents do not always long for the right things. The growth and wisdom they need will also reshape what they long for. Like them, church needs to mature in its longing. In its eschatological imagination, church has often indulged an adolescent vision of the privilege, power, and security of adulthood. It has yearned for a "maturity" that transcends creatureliness and erases uncertainty and incompleteness. Church has longed for "an ersatz universality, a large-scale tribalism with Christ as source and guarantor of the authoritative and comprehensive system of meaning purveyed by the Church."[10] In the modern West especially, ecclesial longing has been infected by an imperial progressivism, which seeks to gain increasing earthly power and influence over other lands and peoples. Just as "the West came to conceive of itself as

---

8. Janet Martin Soskice, "The Ends of Man and the Future of God," in *The End of the World and the Ends of God: Science and Theology on Eschatology*, ed. John Polkinghorne and Michael Welker (Harrisburg, PA: Trinity Press International, 2000), 86.

9. John Calvin, commentary on Eph. 4:14, in *Calvin's New Testament Commentaries*, vol. 11, ed. David W. Torrance and Thomas F. Torrance, trans. T. H. L. Parker (Grand Rapids: Eerdmans, 1965), 182-83.

10. Rowan Williams, "The Finality of Christ," in *On Christian Theology* (Oxford: Blackwell, 2000), 100.

an eschaton—the Utopian path and goal of progress for the world," so the Western church also yearned to be the acme of human virtue and truth.[11] Church's yearning for God to be "all in all" (1 Cor. 15:28) has transmogrified into a longing for its own finality.

By contrast, an ordinary-time ecclesiology insists on a form of ecclesial longing that acknowledges the hallmarks of creaturehood: provisionality and lack of historical closure. This lack of closure is dramatically represented within the church's own story by the continuing existence of the Jewish people and God's abiding faithfulness to them. Christian supersessionism represents a longing for a historical completeness that arrogantly forgets its origins in the particular patterns of God's mercy. Gentile Christians are latecomers to the promises of Israel (Rom. 9:4). They receive their identity by being grafted into those who came before them. Their longing should not seek to erase the particulars of their derivative and dependent religious history or the steadfast promises of God. God is the creator of all, and God continues to heal and bless outside the boundaries of church. Church is not the end of God's ways, and should not fasten its longing on its own earthly success and security, however that is defined. The maturity church longs for is "the measure of the full stature of Christ" (Eph. 4:13), whose life was the antithesis of insular, self-important religiosity. Part of Christian longing is for God to reshape our longing away from self-justification and presumption.

Christian hope is in a God beyond the reach of our calculations and control. Dietrich Bonhoeffer compared the season of Advent to life in a prison cell: "One waits, hopes, does this or that—ultimately negligible things—the door is locked and can only be opened *from the outside*."[12] Christ's coming does not happen on our schedule or according to our fantasies of what this will mean for the community of his followers. But Christ has indeed come. That assurance keeps church from falling into despair or complacency in its longing. Accepting its incompleteness and inability to bring about the fulfillment of its own life, church is better able to embrace the future that Christ holds open for us. "Come quickly, Lord Jesus!"

---

11. J. Kameron Carter, "An Unlikely Convergence: W. E. B. Du Bois, Karl Barth, and the Problem of the Imperial God-Man," *CR: The New Centennial Review* 11 (2011): 173.

12. Bonhoeffer, *Letters and Papers from Prison*, 188 (italics in original).

CHAPTER 8

Giving

*You open your hand, satisfying the desire of every
living thing.*

—Psalm 145:16

At Christmastime, Christians celebrate the gift of what they have longed for. And what a wondrous gift it is! The one who came forth from "the womb of the Father" now grows in Mary's womb.[1] The God in whom "we live and move and have our being" (Acts 17:28) now lives and moves in our world as one of us. In the Christ child the goods of God's own life are made ours. This gift is too great for us to make sense of. It overwhelms our categories, breaking open the earthly boundaries of what we imagine to be possible (Luke 1:37). No wonder that in the birth stories in Matthew and Luke the human response to this news is fear and trembling. In the gift of this baby the floodgates of God's gratuitous love swing open, sweeping us into a drama whose frame of meaning is beyond what we can understand or manage.

Love's pure light enters a world shrouded in darkness, a world full of violence and threat. Each year, as Christians welcome this gift anew, we acknowledge the continuing pain and brokenness of our world. Indeed, our own losses and regrets often seem magnified during this season. Because of the circular rhythms of Christian life, longing for the gift of the Christ

---

1. Eleventh Council of Toledo (675), in *The Christian Faith in the Doctrinal Documents of the Catholic Church*, ed. J. Neuner and J. Dupuis (New York: Alba House, 1982), 103.

child and receiving it are not strictly sequential. With Isaiah and Simeon, church declares, "our eyes have seen your salvation" (Luke 2:30). Yet, as Bonhoeffer comments in a Christmas meditation, "even the fulfillment of all promise and all proper expectation has only begun. Even the time of fulfillment is a long time of waiting."[2] An ordinary-time ecclesiology makes space for both celebrating the gift of Christ and acknowledging our longing for the perfect fulfillment of this gift in a world of hope, joy, love, and peace.

Our giving as Christians is predicated on this unspeakably great gift. We have done nothing to deserve it, and we are still discovering the scope of its transformative power in our lives. To this divine gift, there is no remotely adequate human return, no possible reciprocation or exchange. The only answer we can make, as Rowan Williams observes, is "some faint fumbling echo of that very gratuity and pointlessness itself."[3] In a Christmas sermon, Williams turns our attention to the nativity scene in the fifteenth-century *Second Shepherd's Play*, in which three shepherds present their gifts to the infant Jesus. Their address to him mixes exalted theological language with familiar terms of endearment: "Hail, sovereign saviour. . . . Hail, little tiny mop!"[4] Unlike the magi, the shepherds do not bring what are by human standards noble and valuable gifts. Instead, they present the maker of all things with cherries, a bird, and a tennis ball. All our giving to God is like this: tiny, useless gifts to the God who needs nothing.

Yet, it is right to give God our thanks and praise. Kathryn Tanner notes that "it is a mistake to collapse giving whether or not there is a return into giving that has no return."[5] God gives to us unconditionally. But God also welcomes our response, eager for us to become givers in turn. Giving is

2. Dietrich Bonhoeffer, *Theological Education Underground: 1937–1940*, Dietrich Bonhoeffer Works, vol. 15 (Minneapolis: Fortress, 2012), 22.

3. Rowan Williams, "Christmas Gifts," in *A Ray of Darkness: Sermons and Reflections* (Cambridge, MA: Cowley, 1995), 23.

4. Quoted in Williams, "Christmas Gifts," 23.

5. Kathryn Tanner, *Economy of Grace* (Minneapolis: Fortress, 2005), 71. There is an impressive array of contemporary theological reflection on the concept of gift. In addition to Tanner, my discussion is particularly indebted to J. Todd Billings and Kenneth L. Schmitz: see Billings, *Calvin, Participation, and the Gift* (Oxford: Oxford University Press, 2007); and Schmitz, *The Gift: Creation* (Milwaukee: Marquette University Press, 1982).

one of the regular rhythms of life in the Spirit. In giving praise to God, we draw on our creaturely resources, making new and making do with the raw materials and cultural patterns around us. Our most extravagant and beautiful ways of glorifying God are but tiny reflections of God's own refulgent, glorious beauty. We give to God, not because God needs our gifts, and not out of a sense of obligation, but from an overflowing joy in God's grace.

Christmas is a season of giving gifts. Like the candles and evergreen wreaths of Christmastime, gift-giving is a custom Christians borrowed from others and repurposed. Still, it is wholly fitting that the gift of the Christ child prompts our giving response, both in praise to God and in generosity to each other. Even people who do not usually have much use for church are drawn into the beauty and wonder of Christmas. Christians assemble their musicians and deck their halls to welcome those on the periphery of their communities who still know some of the songs and who come to light candles and hear once again the story of a gift that transcends the transactions and calculations of our daily lives. Even when social jockeying and consumerism mar Christmas gift-giving, a sense of surprise, gratitude, play, and celebration still breaks through. The lavishness of God's giving turns us toward each other with hands open to give and receive. Through the power of the Spirit, church aims to be a community of praise to God and open-handed service to others.

The Gifts of the Creator

In the incarnation, God comes as a creature to creatures. A wisdom ecclesiology sets the divine giving celebrated at Christmas within the larger framework of the unfathomable generosity of God the Creator. As I noted in chapter 1, creation is the original grace of God's economy, a divine act of giving that, like the gift of Christmas, bursts through all our conventional notions of gift exchange. God's gift-giving relationship with us is what gives us being and sustains our lives. There is in God a "reservoir of created goodness that includes an infinity of possibilities that will never be realized."[6] The

6. Schmitz, The Gift: Creation, 21.

doctrine of creation underscores our radical contingency as creatures and thus as givers. This recognition yields a sense of mystery and awe before God and before each other. Our very existence as creatures is a precious gift, and our own modest giving is an appropriate response.

In his reflections on creation, Thomas Aquinas insists that God "alone is the most perfectly liberal giver, because He does not act for His own profit, but only out of His own goodness."[7] The world is not an investment on which God demands a good return. God is the comprehensive principle of all being. God gives us life, a good that is not due to us in any way, since creation is the act of gratuitous love that constitutes us as subjects in the first place. The categories of anthropological discussions of gift-giving thus fail to capture the unique dynamics between Creator and creature. Neither unilateral giving by one party to a passive recipient nor the reciprocal exchange of gifts between them adequately portrays the relationship between human and divine giving. As Todd Billings points out, both "the terms 'reciprocity' and 'passivity' imply an [inappropriate] exteriority in divine-human relations."[8] Instead, God institutes the whole order in which we as creatures are able to give back to God something of what we have already received from God's hand. All our gifts to God, small as they are, rest on this absolute creaturely dependence. They are gifts empowered by the same Spirit who was in Jesus and who now fills us. This dependence on God might seem to threaten the integrity and agency of human creatures, but it is in fact the ground for our genuine agency. All our giving to God and to others is situated within this unfathomable divine liberality.

As creatures, we are receivers before we are givers; all our earthly giving takes place within the interdependent order of human and nonhuman creatures that God has instituted. Our dependence on God is mediated through our dependence on our fellow creatures. From our birth until our death, receiving is a fundamental category of creaturehood. Acknowledging this receiving and responding appropriately is part of the creaturely wisdom God calls us to cultivate. We live as members of what Wendell Berry calls "the

---

7. Thomas Aquinas, *Summa Theologiae*, part 1, ques. 44, art. 4, rep. obj. 1, in *Basic Writings of Saint Thomas Aquinas*, ed. Anton C. Pegis (New York: Random House, 1945), 1:432.
8. J. Todd Billings, "John Milbank's Theology of the 'Gift' and Calvin's Theology of Grace: A Critical Comparison," *Modern Theology* 21, no. 1 (January 2005): 92.

Great Economy" of earthly life: he observes that "we can presume that we are outside the membership that includes us, but that presumption only damages the membership—and ourselves, of course, along with it."[9] Living as ruthless takers in this interdependent economy is self-deluding and ultimately self-destructive. Part of Christian giving is learning to live in sustainable ways with our fellow creatures.

Within the narrower sphere of human interactions we are also receivers before we are givers. As Kenneth Schmitz points out, "human life is impossible without the web of non-reciprocal, unique but mostly anonymous giving and receiving."[10] The nonreciprocity of this complex, intergenerational web means that exchange cannot function as the primary model for human giving. Our cultural and linguistic traditions, for example, imperfect as they are, are gifts received from a long temporal chain of benefactors, most of whom remain anonymous to us. There is no way for us to "reciprocate," except to use their gifts well and pass them on to others. Likewise, church lives by the gifts it has received from mostly anonymous others, from buildings and musical styles to sacred texts and sacramental traditions. There is no way for church to give back to the original donors of these gifts. Instead, church "gives forward," using these gifts gratefully for the praise of God and the benefit of other creatures. Our giving to others is always couched in a web of gifts we have received from others. There is an indispensable generosity to creaturely life. We respond to God's manifold gifts to us by becoming mediators of God's gifts to others.

Wise Giving

Without attention to creaturely fallibility and finitude, theological understandings of human giving tend to float above the texture of real life. Biblical Wisdom literature, with its keen sense of God's creative presence and its stout realism about the limitations and vulnerabilities of communal human life, is a neglected resource for Christian theologies of gift. The Wisdom books insist that all good things ultimately come to us from the hand of

---

9. Wendell Berry, *Home Economics* (New York: North Point, 1987), 75.
10. Schmitz, *The Gift*, 56.

God (Eccles. 2:24–25). Within the creaturely life established by this divine generosity, our own giving is essential for general human flourishing. We are vulnerable, interdependent creatures living in a world in which "time and chance happen to all" (Eccles. 9:11). The *do ut des* (I give so that you will give) model of human giving is drastically inadequate in such a risky and unpredictable world. All our giving occurs in a framework that is too big for us to manage or control, and so we give without knowing the outcome. "Send out your bread upon the waters," Qohelet counsels, "for after many days you will get it back" (Eccles. 11:1). Qohelet's point is that this communal sharing is not to be done in a calculating way, but freely and generously. We give, not being able to foresee when or what we will get back. Yet, in a more general way, our giving does have an expectable result: generosity breeds generosity, forming a society in which gifts circulate freely, enriching all. The apostle Paul reflects this wisdom orientation when he exhorts the Corinthians to contribute to the collection for Jerusalem so that there will be "a fair balance between your present abundance and their need, so that their abundance may be for your need" (2 Cor. 8:14). The goal of this giving was that "the one who had much did not have too much, and the one who had little did not have too little" (Exod. 16:18; 2 Cor. 8:15). The Wisdom books' exhortations to give are a reflection of creaturely wisdom about what is required of us for the sake of living well in society with others. For Israel's sages, the purity of the giver's intentions is not the primary issue. Human survival and well-being depends on a circulation of gifts. Giving to those in need is thus wise, not just good.

On the other hand, biblical wisdom is clear-eyed about the pitfalls of human giving and receiving. Gift-giving among vulnerable, fallible creatures is easily corrupted. Israel's sages are alert to the mixed motives that often lie behind human giving and to the dangers of accepting gifts from wicked, foolish, or powerful people. "Do not eat the bread of the stingy," Proverbs warns. " 'Eat and drink!' they say to you; but they do not mean it" (Prov. 23:6–7). The Wisdom books also recognize that gift-giving does not obviate the need for hard work and honest business dealings. Alongside our giving, our forms of labor and commerce can also be ways of responding to God's gifts and contributing to human flourishing. The Wisdom books celebrate the liberality of God's gifts, while they maintain a realism about the constraints and ambiguities of human giving.

Church in ordinary time must also be clear-eyed about both the necessity and the risks of human giving. It should not promote a model of Christian giving that is dismissive of—or impatient with—our creatureliness. God's giving knows no ending, but ours is hemmed in by our creaturely finitude. As Kenneth Schmitz notes, our existence as givers is indelibly marked with "discontinuity and contingency, with risk, vulnerability, and surprise."[11] Theologians should not jump too quickly to the perfections of God's eternal triune life as a model for our giving and receiving. Human giving, unlike God's, is creaturely, and thus limited by constraints of time, resources, energy, and geography. We remain needy givers.

Shel Silverstein's *The Giving Tree* is often allegorized as a moral lesson for children about giving.[12] In this story a beautiful apple tree, disturbingly referred to with feminine pronouns, gives of herself to a demanding boy. She first gives in sustainable ways: her shed leaves and ripe apples. But then she gives her branches and finally her trunk, till at last she is reduced to a dead stump. A tree that should have lived a hundred years is destroyed in one human generation. From the perspective of a wisdom ecclesiology, this is a parable of ecological rapacity, not a paradigm of Christian giving. Kathryn Tanner warns against a notion of gift that demands the diminishment of self, requiring "the superhuman, heroic efforts of isolated individuals."[13] Her warning can be expanded to the dangers of making sacrificial giving the paradigm for communal Christian life, especially when those with social power demand this kind of giving from weak and vulnerable members of the community. Communal expectations for giving can intensify unjust relations within human communities. Children of hosts, for example, go hungry so that important guests will be well fed. Spouses are sent back to their batterers to be an example of self-giving love. This does not mean that Christians should never emulate the churches of Macedonia, who "voluntarily gave according to their means, and even beyond their means" (2 Cor. 8:3). But it does mean that we should acknowledge our creaturely vulnerability, and that concern for the welfare of "the least" among us should shape Christian patterns of giving.

11. Schmitz, *The Gift*, 44.
12. Shel Silverstein, *The Giving Tree* (New York: Harper and Row, 1964).
13. Tanner, *Economy of Grace*, 75–76.

Living in the Light of Christ

"Arise, shine, for your light is come, and the glory of the LORD has risen upon you!" (Isa. 60:1). Church lives in the light of Christ's coming. In its giving, it leans into an eschatological vision of universal communion in which all creation rejoices together in God's boundless generosity. Church in ordinary time aims to be a community whose life gives life to others. In its joyful giving it seeks to offer a faint fumbling echo of the extraordinary gift it has received in Christ.

Church leans into the good news of Christmas with both feet planted in God's earth. For now, Christians must be concerned with good working conditions and fair wages, with sustainable energy policies and social structures that provide well for the vulnerable and marginalized. Concern for these matters is a way of acknowledging God's gifts and distributing them to our fellow creatures. But these social goods are not the hope of the world. The hope of the world has come in Jesus, and this unspeakably great gift promises to upset the political and economic order as we know it, and even as we can imagine it. Mary rejoices in a God who scatters the proud in the thoughts of their hearts and brings down the powerful from their thrones, who lifts up the lowly and fills the hungry with good things (Luke 1:51–53). The earthly injustice and suffering that can block our experience of God's gifts do not get the last word; we trust that in Christ the failures and vulnerabilities of our creaturely giving do not get the last word either. In its giving, church points ahead of itself to the fulfillment of all promise in Christ.

There is a short stretch of liturgical ordinary time between the end of the Christmas season and the beginning of Lent. This is a perfect time for church to practice being a community of giving, in which each person's gifts are welcomed and are used for the flourishing of the whole. Like the shepherds, we present our creaturely gifts to God and to each other, trusting that by the power of the Spirit they are taken up into the vast generosity of God and will not return to us empty.

CHAPTER 9

Suffering

*For my sighing comes like my bread, and my groanings are
poured out like water.*

—Job 3:24

At the center of Christian faith is the cross, a reminder of Christ's suffering, forsakenness, and death. Though Christian theology sometimes
yearns to draw a straight line from cross to resurrection, a progression from
suffering to glory that does not look back, the rhythms of church life are
more honest about the texture of human experience. Lent is a season of suffering. Every year church walks through the valley of the shadow of death
with Christ, sharing in his sufferings and grieving the forces at death that are
still at work in the world and in its own life. In many Christian traditions,
Lent is accompanied by powerful corporate rituals: stations of the cross,
fasting, lament, ashes of repentance. These practices are a means of putting
on the vulnerable flesh of Christ, of carrying his suffering and death around
in our bodies (2 Cor. 4:10). In Lent we hide our alleluias for a season, abandoning the pretense that all is right with us and with our world. The Easter
joy that will follow enters a world that still bears the wounds of the cross.

The suffering of Lent is ordinarily situated within a theological narrative
of sin and redemption. In the face of the crucified Christ, his followers see
the fate of human beings left to themselves. Christ ends up on the cross because that is where humanity is, trapped in webs of violence, oppression, and
enmity. Entering into creaturely solidarity with us, incarnate Wisdom takes

on our alienation from God and each other. The cross is our assurance that no one is beyond the reach of God's healing and transforming forgiveness. For church, the suffering of Lent comes from the honest acknowledgment of our ongoing need for this healing and transformation. The cross confronts us with the reality that sin and its death-dealing power still surround us and live within us. Church cries out for deliverance from bondage to the powers and principalities that impoverish and corrode our common life. Acknowledging and dying to this sin involves suffering. According to the Scots Confession, the Spirit's work of sanctification is long and painful: "The sons of God fight against sin; sob and mourn when they find themselves tempted to do evil; and, if they fall, rise again with earnest and unfeigned repentance."[1] New life in the Spirit lies on the other side of our death to sin.

Lent involves personal and communal stock-taking and rituals of repentance, but it is not solely inward-looking. Becoming attuned to Christ's sufferings and our own need for redemption opens us toward a suffering world that is also crying out for deliverance. The Lamb of God whose mercy Christians implore is the One who takes away the sin of the whole world. Drawing close to Christ requires drawing close to the suffering of others. Dietrich Bonhoeffer says that "it is not a religious act that makes someone a Christian, but rather sharing in God's suffering in the worldly life."[2] Church is not called to this role because its own redemption is complete and can now be extended to others. We are pulled along by the Spirit to share in the suffering of the world because that is where Jesus is.

According to Bonhoeffer, even when the world inflicts suffering on Christians, their role is to remain in solidarity with it:

> We do not abandon it; we do not repudiate, despise, or condemn it. Instead we call it back to God, we give it hope, we lay our hand on it and say: "[M]ay God's blessing come upon you, may God renew you; be blessed, world created by God, you who belong to your Creator and Redeemer."[3]

1. The Scots Confession 3.13, in *The Constitution of the Presbyterian Church (USA)*, part 1, *Book of Confessions, Study Edition* (Louisville: Geneva Press, 1999), 39.

2. Dietrich Bonhoeffer, *Letters and Papers from Prison*, Dietrich Bonhoeffer Works, vol. 8 (Minneapolis: Fortress, 2010), 480.

3. Dietrich Bonhoeffer, *Conspiracy and Imprisonment, 1940–1945*, Dietrich Bonhoeffer Works, vol. 16 (Minneapolis: Fortress, 2006), 632.

Bonhoeffer is clear that we "are not Christ, nor are we called to redeem the world through our own deed and our own suffering."[4] Instead, Christians are to bestow the same blessing on the world that they yearn for themselves: to be called back to God and renewed. Church gives especially powerful witness to Christ's merciful presence when it penitently acknowledges its role in the suffering of others, such as repudiating its teaching of contempt against Jews, or seeking to make concrete amends for its active role in the enslavement of others. Lent is a season in which church acknowledges its commonality with a sinful world, as God's beloved creatures in need of redemption.

Creaturely Dimensions of Suffering

A wisdom ecclesiology broadens this Lenten identity by exploring the creaturely dimensions of suffering. The suffering of church and world overflows the categories of sin and redemption. Suffering is not only the consequence of our sin; it is also a result of our creaturely limitations and vulnerability. Sin and creaturely finitude are all tangled up together in human suffering, and this more complex reality must be taken into account. Some of the most damaging Christian theology has come from attempts to confine all suffering within the orbit of sin and redemption. When this happens, the temptation is to glorify human suffering as intrinsically redemptive or to rationalize it as a punishment for sin. But much of our suffering, both personal and communal, does not conform to these rubrics. Suffering that flows from injustice, natural disaster, or disease is not heroic or freely chosen, and it should not be glorified. Suffering often simply happens to us, a mark of our vulnerability and incompleteness as creatures. While sin resides in all of us, and while it lives in sedimented form in our histories and structures, it is wrong to insist that suffering is always the direct consequence of sin, our own or someone else's. Suffering defies our algorithms of moral desert. For a more adequate account of church's suffering, it is helpful to turn once again to biblical wisdom.

The book of Job is a vehement protest against a theology that appeals to sin and its consequences to give a full explanation of suffering. Within a

4. Bonhoeffer, *Letters and Papers from Prison*, 49.

theological framework that makes all suffering a matter of human sin and divine justice, the central question between Job and his friends is whether Job's suffering is deserved or not. Yet within the book's narrative frame, the suffering Job endures is largely the result of natural forces: his children are lost in storms, lightning destroys his cattle, and disease makes his life miserable. As Terence Fretheim points out, the theological questions Job's suffering raises are primarily about "the nature of God's creation and God's continuing relationship to it."[5] Job's friends Eliphaz and Bildad portray the created world as a wonderful and precise bit of divine engineering, in which cause and effect are neatly predictable in human life. Job protests that view: it is not always the case that we reap what we sow. God's speech from the whirlwind depicts the creation as beautiful and good, but also wild and dangerous, beyond human control and understanding. Creaturely life within such a world has inherent and unavoidable risks, and God's people receive no guarantees that they will evade the suffering endemic to creaturely life. Rather than attempt to "make sense" of suffering—as a punishment for sin or lack of faith, as part of some perfect divine plan, as something that will be compensated for by heavenly rewards and punishments—an account of church in ordinary time insists with Job that in suffering we run up against the limits of our creaturely wisdom. Once we put aside misguided attempts at theological explanation, our faithful response to our own suffering and that of others will take many forms, including repentance, lament, and work for justice and healing, all of them buoyed by trust in Christ's merciful presence.

Church has no failsafe way to guard itself against creaturely suffering. For an ordinary-time ecclesiology, part of the repentance of Lent involves relinquishing resentment about our creaturely limits and fantasies about ecclesial power and control. Lent demands an ecclesiology of the cross. In Tertullian's memorable phrase, flesh is "the pivot of salvation."[6] Salvation happens through a communion of vulnerable flesh, both Christ's flesh and ours; vulnerability to suffering and death is thus inextricably part of church's story. To be a community of Christ's followers is to trust that his saving power is

---

5. Terence E. Fretheim, *Creation Untamed: The Bible, God, and Natural Disasters* (Grand Rapids: Baker Academic, 2010), 74.

6. Tertullian, *Treatise on the Resurrection* 8, trans. Ernest Evans (London: SPCK, 1960), 25.

made perfect in weakness, not that God will always remove the thorns that afflict us (2 Cor. 12:7, 9). Yet theologies of glory remain a temptation in ecclesiology. Teachings of ecclesial indefectibility have been construed as ensuring church's triumph over all obstacles. Missional ecclesiologies have been predicated on Christianity's continuous growth and expansion. Prosperity gospels have assured the faithful of victorious Christian life on earth. Many accounts of church do not know what to do with ecclesial failure and decline. A wisdom ecclesiology attempts to make theological space for acknowledging these concrete realities and the suffering that accompanies them.

The Church Vulnerable

As Augustine has taught us, we are not self-sufficient creatures. We are restless, incomplete beings who necessarily inhabit and reach out to a world beyond ourselves. Jonathan Lear points out that "*a world* is not merely the environment in which we move about; it is that over which we lack omnipotent control, that about which we may be mistaken in significant ways, that which may intrude upon us, that which may outstrip the concepts with which we seek to understand it."[7] Like other creaturely communities, church inhabits a world in this way, which means that the church militant is also the church vulnerable—vulnerable to ecological catastrophe, to cultural upheavals of all kinds, to the consequences of its own foolish and sinful choices. To sustain its life, church cannot help but open itself to the world around it, but that opening has inherent risks: it may choose a destructive path, it may get hurt, the world may change in ways that present insuperable challenges to its way of life.

Rachel Muers notes that contemporary environmental concern addresses "the increasing likelihood of total or partial failure to maintain a habitable environment for many living creatures, including quite possibly the human creature."[8] Church cannot expect to be exempt from the suffering associated with significant unraveling of social and ecological systems. Its creaturely life

---

7. Jonathan Lear, *Radical Hope: Ethics in the Face of Cultural Devastation* (Cambridge, MA: Harvard University Press, 2008), 120.

8. Rachel Muers, "The Holy Spirit, the Voice of Nature and Environmental Prophecy," *Scottish Journal of Theology* 67, no. 3 (2014): 337.

is bound up with that of others, and cannot flourish apart from them. This acknowledgment does not justify passivity or complacency in the face of ecological challenges. But it also does not assume that human agency or God's providential care guarantees that ecological disaster will be averted. Muers maintains that the appropriate Christian theological response must take the form of "a steadfast refusal to deny limitation, vulnerability, death and loss."[9] Within a wisdom ecclesiology, this refusal is a form of Lenten mortification, a recognition of the power of death that still hangs over creaturely life.

Jonathan Lear has examined the cultural devastation of the Crow people in North America at the end of the nineteenth century, once the great herds of buffalo that had anchored their way of life disappeared. His analysis has import for other communities that are, like church, also vulnerable to cultural collapse.[10] Every culture depends on the continued viability of its conceptual resources: the assumption that the current field of possibilities will remain stable and that the members of that culture will be able to judge success or failure in its terms. Like other communities, church is situated within a certain field of cultural possibilities and it cannot simply transpose itself into another cultural location. As we saw in chapter 6, church is always in the process of making new and making do with the cultural resources around it. Church is also dependent on the material resources of its social location: water, land, food, and some measure of peace and economic opportunity. When the material and cultural resources that sustain the church in a given place dry up, categories of life that were once meaningful can become uninhabitable.

In general, Lear notes, human cultures are not very good at conceiving the possibility of their own devastation. "By and large a culture will not teach its young: 'These are ways in which you can succeed, and these are ways in which you will fail; these are dangers you might face, and here are opportunities; these acts are shameful, and these are worthy of honor—and, oh yes, one more thing, this entire structure of evaluating the world might cease to make sense.' "[11] The book of Proverbs models a dependence on ways of life that are still vibrant and functioning. Ecclesiastes is one of the few books in

9. Muers, "The Holy Spirit," 339.

10. Ted A. Smith draws these connections in "Theories of Practice," in *The Wiley Blackwell Companion to Practical Theology*, ed. Bonnie J. Miller-McLemore (Oxford: Blackwell, 2012), 244–54.

11. Lear, *Radical Hope*, 83.

the Bible that is willing to stare into the void and ask, What happens when a whole way of life falls apart?

Cultural devastation is unfortunately not a new thing for church; in fact, it is a recurrent feature of church history. Examples come readily to mind. The first centuries of Christianity were concentrated around the edges of the Mediterranean. North Africa used to be the Christian heartland, home to the most sophisticated theological reflection and the best libraries of Christian texts. Some of the most prominent names in the early church—Cyprian, Tertullian, and Augustine—were North Africans. The Christian faith flourished there long before it made its way up to the barbarian tribes in northern Europe. But few traces of the North African church remain today. The conditions that made for ecclesial flourishing in that time and place gradually disappeared, and the ecclesial center of gravity shifted northward toward Europe. As we now know, that shift in Christianity's center of gravity toward Western Europe was itself a temporary phenomenon. The story of church on earth is not a glorious story of continuous progress and expansion; it is a Lenten story of continual death and rebirth. Andrew Walls notes that there seems to be "some inherent fragility, some built-in vulnerability" implied in Christian faith. Christianity's growth over the centuries has been serial, not progressive. The Christian faith advances, but it also recedes.[12] Furthermore, it repeatedly recedes from the centers of strength and advances from the weak areas at the periphery. A wisdom ecclesiology seeks to make theological sense of the actual history of church, with its theological triumphs and failures, its geographical expansions and recessions, and its recurrent vulnerability to cultural and material devastation.

The Suffering That Remains

The growing theological recognition of the lasting effects of creaturely trauma has helped deepen Christian accounts of human existence and salvation but has not yet made much headway in ecclesiology.[13] A Lenten ac-

---

12. Andrew Walls, "Christianity in the Non-Western World: A Study in the Serial Nature of Christian Expansion," in *Studies in World Christianity* 1, no. 1 (1995): 1–25.

13. Shelly Rambo, *Spirit and Trauma: A Theology of Remaining* (Louisville: Westmin-

count of church has to acknowledge the earthly suffering that remains in the wake of devastating losses. Traumas such as war, epidemics of disease, persecution, or the reverberations from ecclesial collaborations with evil leave lasting scars. The healing and hope that the Spirit brings do not reverse the passage of time and bring back church life exactly as it once was. Nor does the Spirit catapult church over its suffering directly into resurrection life; instead, the Spirit remains with us as we continue to hurt and search for healing. Hans Urs von Balthasar suggests that Holy Saturday, understood as the time of Christ's descent into hell, is key to Christian understandings of redemption. Otherwise, he notes, "the danger is very real that we, as spectators of a drama beyond our comprehension, will simply wait until the scene changes."[14] Waiting until the scene changes to Easter glory is not an option for church as it confronts forces of suffering and death that leave lasting marks on its life.

Responding to suffering by simply waiting till the scene changes reflects the assumption that Christian life is best understood as a drama that moves inexorably toward a happy ending. The reality of trauma challenges the adequacy of this understanding as a guide to Christian communal life. The fracturing of persons and communities by trauma can destroy the ability to make sense of our existence via a cohesive narrative. Perhaps here, too, the genre of biblical wisdom, with its sturdy resistance to a narrative structure, is a neglected resource for speaking from and to trauma. Ellen Davis reports the testimony of a Vietnam War chaplain that Ecclesiastes was "the only part of the Bible that his soldiers were willing to hear."[15] Alongside the biblical genre of lament, the Wisdom books can help church voice the dislocation and lasting wounds that traumatic suffering inflicts.

---

ster John Knox, 2010). "The suffering that remains" is a phrase borrowed from Rambo, *Spirit and Trauma*, 15. See also Serene Jones, *Trauma and Grace: Theology in a Ruptured World* (Louisville: Westminster John Knox, 2009); Flora Keshgegian, *Redeeming Memories: A Theology of Healing and Transformation* (Nashville: Abingdon, 2000); and Jennifer Beste, *God and the Victim: Traumatic Intrusions on Grace and Freedom* (New York: Oxford University Press, 2007).

14. Hans Urs von Balthasar, *Mysterium Paschale*, trans. Aidan Nichols (Grand Rapids: Eerdmans, 1993), 50, quoted in Rambo, *Spirit and Trauma*, 46.

15. Ellen F. Davis, *Proverbs, Ecclesiastes, and the Song of Songs*, Westminster Bible Companion (Louisville: Westminster John Knox, 2000), 159.

As it lives with the suffering that remains, church's assurance is that Jesus also remains. Even though the disciples failed to remain with Jesus in the agony of his dereliction, we trust him to remain with us when the cup of our suffering is not taken away. Relying on the merciful presence of Jesus, church seeks to be a space where the wounds of crucifixion are not denied, where the continuing reality of death and failure and trauma is not covered up, where lament finds a communal home. In our suffering, Jesus walks with us, Jesus hears us, Jesus prays with us.

CHAPTER 10

Rejoicing

> *Let the heavens be glad, and let the earth rejoice;*
> *let the sea roar, and all that fills it;*
> *let the field exult, and everything in it.*
>
> —Psalm 96:11–12

Christ is risen! Church orients its life around this Easter joy. Every Sunday is a little Easter, a celebration of God's vindication of Jesus's entire life and death in raising him from the grave. Every act of worship is a celebration of the living presence of Christ in our midst, a presence that now knows no restrictions of time or space. Easter is the centerpiece of Christian life, a standing call to rejoice in the triumph of life over death, of love over hatred and alienation, of hope over despair. In the strange and surprising story of Jesus's resurrection, church already knows how the story of God's love for us will end, and that establishes joy and gratitude as the fundamental tenor of its common life. Easter is the dawning of God's promised future, and every feast day, every baptism, every confirmation and ordination, even every funeral, is a whisper of the new life that is already starting to unfold. Easter is God's seal that the last word on creaturely life will be peace and praise, and the joy of that hope is already seeping into the present.

Church's rejoicing is a sharing in God's economy of joy. We rejoice in the joyful freedom and constancy of God's dealings with us, even in the midst of our suffering and sin. Our rejoicing is a sharing in the boundless good pleasure of the triune God, whose life-giving love for creation is never exhausted.

This means that Christian joy is not an escapist joy that denies the present suffering and brokenness of creation. It is not a vengeful joy that divides and alienates God's creatures from each other. In one of his circular letters to his former students and colleagues at Finkenwalde, Dietrich Bonhoeffer meditates on Isaiah 35:10 ("Everlasting joy shall be upon their heads"). "The joy of God," he writes, "has gone through the poverty of the manger and the agony of the cross, that is why it is invincible, irrefutable." When our joy is a sharing in this divine joy, "it does not deny the anguish, when it is there, but finds God in the midst of it, in fact precisely there; it does not deny grave sin but finds forgiveness precisely in this way; it looks death straight in the eye, but it finds life precisely within it."[1] This is the clear-eyed yet hopeful rejoicing that church is called to: it does not deny the realities of suffering, sin, and death, but it sets them within a framework of confidence in the triumph of God's grace in Jesus Christ.

The Genesis of Joy

An account of church in ordinary time recognizes that Christian rejoicing does not begin with the season of Easter. That is because the economy of God's joy is not bounded by the story of God's victory over sin and death in Jesus Christ, no matter how central that story is to Christian self-understanding. The divine economy of joy begins with the God who "calls into existence the things that do not exist" (Rom. 4:17) and who continues to sustain all living things. We are first of all the object of God's delight simply in our integrity and particularity as the creatures God made us to be. Proverbs 8:22–31 depicts Woman Wisdom at God's side during the creation of the world, and ends with her jubilant declaration:

I was daily his delight,
rejoicing before him always,
rejoicing in his inhabited world
and delighting in the human race. (Prov. 8:30b–31)

1. Dietrich Bonhoeffer, *Conspiracy and Imprisonment, 1940–1945*, Dietrich Bonhoeffer Works, vol. 16 (Minneapolis: Fortress, 2006), 378.

This rejoicing and delight in creaturely life has its roots in God's perfect generosity. From vast constellations to tiny minnows, creation is for the creature's sake, not for God's. God delights in bestowing life on what did not have to be, and Woman Wisdom rejoices in this enactment of God's boundless goodness. To share in God's economy of joy is to join Woman Wisdom in joyful praise for the sheer gift of creaturely life.

Church's Easter rejoicing in God's gifts of reconciliation and resurrection hope does not take the joy of creaturely existence for granted. Creaturely existence is not a given but a gift, and thus an ongoing cause for our rejoicing. "He commanded and they were created," says the psalmist. That is reason enough to call sun, moon, stars—and church—to rejoice (Ps. 148:3–5). Rejoicing in God's creativity is only appropriate, because this is the source and sustenance of the creaturely life needed for us to offer praise in the first place. The joy of Easter crowns this earthly joy but does not replace it. With Bonhoeffer, an ordinary-time ecclesiology insists that the Christian hope of resurrection does not mute our praise for the gift of earthly life; rather, it "refers people to their life on earth in a wholly new way."[2] Resurrection hope calls church to join with all people who worship the Creator of heaven and earth—indeed, with all the earth's creatures—in making "a joyful noise to the Lord" (Ps. 100:1a).

Though Woman Wisdom makes special mention of the human race in Proverbs 8:31, the joy of the Creator reaches far beyond our particular species. In Job's marvelous depiction of God's delight in and attentive care for creatures (chapters 38–41), human beings are not at the center of the picture. God delights even in monsters like Behemoth and Leviathan, fearsome forces of chaos that overwhelm all attempts at human control (Job 40:15–41:34). To share in the economy of God's joy is to expand our horizon beyond the story of human salvation and even beyond what benefits us directly as human creatures to embrace a much bigger cosmic story. We do not rejoice only in God's gifts to us, as if the whole divine economy were oriented exclusively toward our needs. Our human creaturehood does not set the terms for God's joyful relationship to the rest of creation. "Is it by your wisdom that the hawk soars?" God asks Job. "Do you give the horse its might?" (Job 39:19, 26). In its

---

2. Dietrich Bonhoeffer, *Letters and Papers from Prison*, Dietrich Bonhoeffer Works, vol. 8 (Minneapolis: Fortress, 2010), 447.

rejoicing, church cultivates a wonder and delight at evidences of God's wisdom and generosity toward all creation. Christian ecological commitment rightly flows from praise for the Creator of all things.[3]

Our reflexive anthropocentrism is further destabilized by the biblical insistence that human beings do not rejoice all by themselves: our fellow creatures join us in praising God's goodness. It would be more accurate to say that we join them. In Karl Barth's lovely image, humanity is "like a late-comer slipping shamefacedly into creation's choir in heaven and earth, which has never ceased its praise."[4] Just as Proverbs lifts up the lowly ant and badger as examples of wisdom (Prov. 30:25–26), so the psalmist lifts up the myriad voices of our fellow creatures as models of rejoicing for us to emulate. In the presence of the LORD, "the sea roars, and all that fills it; the floods clap their hands; the hills sing together for joy" (Ps. 98:7–9). Of course, the sea has been roaring and the hills singing together for hundreds of millions of years before human beings, including Christians, joined the chorus. Because of the extravagant goodness of the Creator, church's modest rejoicing is taken up into eons of creaturely praise.

Daniel Hardy and David Ford note that "creation's praise is not an extra, an addition to what it is, but the shining of its being, the overflowing significance it has in pointing to its Creator simply by being itself."[5] Creation's praise is what creaturely rejoicing in God looks like in the absence of sin. Church yearns for the healing of its creaturehood, so that rejoicing in God becomes "the shining of its being," not some appendage to its life. This is part of our resurrection hope. In the meantime, conscious participation in the rejoicing of our fellow creatures deepens and challenges our own worship of God, putting us in the enormous company of those who already "rejoice in the Lord always" (Phil. 4:4).

Giving thanks is always right and fitting, and church's Easter rejoicing properly finds its place within the larger creaturely polyphony of praise.

---

3. For an example of this theological movement, see Pope Francis's 2015 papal encyclical *Laudato si'*.

4. Karl Barth, *Church Dogmatics*, II/1, ed. G. W. Bromiley and T. F. Torrance (Edinburgh: T&T Clark, 1957), 648.

5. Daniel W. Hardy and David F. Ford, *Jubilate: Theology in Praise* (London: Darton, Longman and Todd, 1984), 82; see also Richard Bauckham, *The Bible and Ecology: Rediscovering the Community of Creation* (Waco, TX: Baylor University Press, 2010).

Yet church's rejoicing does not reach its terminus in creaturely gratitude for God's gifts, whether those are gifts of creation or gifts of redemption and everlasting life. "God is God," Jonathan Edwards declares, "and distinguished from all other beings, and exalted above 'em, chiefly by his divine beauty."[6] God's joy finds its source in the eternal beauty of God's own life and only derivatively in God's economic work of creation and redemption. The beauty of the creatures created and redeemed by God is, in Edwards's words, "but the reflection of the diffused beams of that Being who hath an infinite fullness of brightness and glory."[7] The perfection of God's life is not established by God's engagement with creatures or by the existence of church, but radiates from the eternal circulation of love and life within the Trinity, which Edwards calls "the supreme harmony of all."[8] In its rejoicing, church rightly revels in God's good gifts, both the gift of creaturely life and the promise of eternal communion with God. But church also points away from itself, rejoicing in the "ancient beauty" of God, which shines irrespective of the acknowledgment or even the existence of creaturely latecomers like itself.[9] This is finally what it means for the Easter church to pray: to be swept up by the power of the Spirit into Jesus's own praise and love to the Father, rejoicing in a communion with God that has no end.

Penultimate and Ultimate

Church lives in the penultimate, knowing that in Christ's resurrection the ultimate has already dawned. How to live faithfully in this tension between the penultimate and the ultimate became a focus of sharp attention in the

6. Jonathan Edwards, *Religious Affections*, ed. John E. Smith, The Works of Jonathan Edwards, vol. 2 (New Haven: Yale University Press, 1959), 298.

7. Jonathan Edwards, *Ethical Writings*, ed. Paul Ramsey, The Works of Jonathan Edwards, vol. 8 (New Haven: Yale University Press, 1989), 550-51.

8. Jonathan Edwards, *The "Miscellanies,"* ed. Thomas A. Schafer, The Works of Jonathan Edwards, vol. 13 (New Haven: Yale University Press, 1994), 329 (no. 182). For an account of Edwards's Trinitarianism, see Amy Plantinga Pauw, *The Supreme Harmony of All: The Trinitarian Theology of Jonathan Edwards* (Grand Rapids: Eerdmans, 2002).

9. Augustine, *Confessions* 10.38, trans. Maria Boulding (Hyde Park, NY: New City Press, 2001), p. 262.

last years of Bonhoeffer's life. In this time between the times, Bonhoeffer urges church to remain in step with God, "drinking the cup of earthly life to the last drop," as Christ did. He insists that "this-worldliness must not be abolished ahead of its time."[10] Church's Easter joy becomes distorted when it leads to the denigration of God's creaturely gifts or presents itself as an escape route out of earthly difficulties into eternity. For now, joy in the resurrection must make its home on earth, leaving room as well for rejoicing in God's earthly gifts.

Church is called to rejoice in penultimate things: bodily life, family, friends, food, work, music, natural beauty, progress toward justice, and so many more are reasons for joy. Church rejoices in the end of a drought, peacemaking among enemies, a promising new therapy for cancer. These things are not in our secure possession or control. They are incomplete and imperfect: they are temporal gifts that expose our creaturely vulnerability and dependence—gifts of the day, vulnerable to being lost at any moment. Joy in these things is the joy commended by Ecclesiastes.[11] Throughout Ecclesiastes, the teacher Qohelet acknowledges and laments the miseries and contingencies of finite creaturehood. Life is a vanity of vanities (Eccles. 1:2; 12:8), and finding joy in it is not propelled by the absence or the denial of life's vanity. Rather, it is predicated on a grateful acknowledgment of our creaturehood. The frustrations and limits that Qohelet has discovered everywhere in human life remain. Joy in God's gifts as Creator is called forth in the midst of them. Poet Wendell Berry catches some of the paradox of this joy when he writes, "Be joyful, even in the face of all the facts."[12] Church in ordinary time is called to this kind of joy.

There are few biblical exhortations to everyday joy as heartfelt as Qohelet's: "Go, eat your bread with enjoyment, and drink your wine with a merry heart; for God has long ago approved what you do" (Eccles. 9:7). Bonhoeffer thought that Christians could benefit from Qohelet's appreciation of God's presence in the ordinary joys of creaturely life. Commenting

10. Bonhoeffer, *Letters and Papers from Prison*, 447.

11. The reflections on Ecclesiastes that follow are drawn from Amy Plantinga Pauw, *Proverbs and Ecclesiastes*, Belief: A Theological Commentary on the Bible (Louisville: Westminster John Knox, 2015), esp. 171–72.

12. Wendell Berry, "Manifesto: The Mad Farmer Liberation Front," in *The Selected Poems of Wendell Berry* (Berkeley, CA: Counterpoint, 1998), 87.

on Ecclesiastes 3, Bonhoeffer writes: "One should find and love God in what God directly gives us." "To say it clearly," he goes on to declare, "that a person in the arms of his wife should long for the hereafter is, to put it mildly, tasteless and in any case is not God's will."[13] God "has made everything suitable for its time" (Eccles. 3:11). Joy in the ultimate promise of everlasting life with God does not require negating the penultimate joys of the present. Christ "takes hold of human beings in the midst of their lives," in their creaturely strength and happiness, not only in their suffering and longing for the world to come.[14] Yet Bonhoeffer is also clear that Christians should eschew "the shallow and banal this-worldliness" of those who seek nothing beyond epicurean pleasures. Christian rejoicing in earthly things is hemmed in by an "ever-present knowledge of death and resurrection."[15]

Easter joy now sounds amidst earthly rejoicing, but earthly rejoicing will not last forever. One day even the sea will stop its roaring. This does not mean that creaturely rejoicing is unfaithful or insignificant. We are temporal creatures, and we do not receive all of God's gifts at once. We are called to rejoice in what God gives us each day, even if those gifts will one day cease. "God will not fail the person who finds his earthly happiness in God and is grateful, in those hours when he is reminded that all earthly things are temporary and that it is good to accustom his heart to eternity."[16] Likewise, God will not fail the church that is grateful for God's earthly gifts.

Church knows that its earthly life will always be imperfect and incomplete. It will not last forever. As church rejoices in penultimate things, it knows that it, too, is penultimate to God's ultimate purposes. Instead of indulging in "wild religious fantasy that is never satisfied with what God gives,"[17] the earthly church rejoices in the penultimate role God has given it. It "drinks the cup of earthly life to the last drop," even as it joins all creation in longing to be raised with Christ from death to imperishable life (1 Cor. 15:42).

13. Bonhoeffer, *Letters and Papers from Prison*, 228.
14. Bonhoeffer, *Letters and Papers from Prison*, 448.
15. Bonhoeffer, *Letters and Papers from Prison*, 485.
16. Bonhoeffer, *Letters and Papers from Prison*, 228.
17. Bonhoeffer, *Letters and Papers from Prison*, 228.

CHAPTER 11

Joining Hands

We carry each other. If we don't have this, what are we?

—ANNE MICHAELS, *Fugitive Pieces*

On Pentecost, church celebrates the Holy Spirit's work of joining. As recounted in Acts 2, faithful Jews from every nation were gathered together in Jerusalem on the day of Pentecost, a harvest festival celebrated on the fiftieth day after Passover. The Holy Spirit came upon them "like the rush of a violent wind" (Acts 2:2), and each of them was able to hear about God's deeds of power in their own language. The Spirit joined together those divided by language, geography, and culture—without erasing their differences. At Pentecost the Spirit was poured out on *all* flesh, and, as a result, unjust social orders that separated and alienated people from each other began to totter. As the prophet Joel testifies, with the coming of the Spirit, both male and female slaves receive the authority to prophesy (Joel 2:28–29; Acts 2:16–18). The power of the Spirit witnessed at Pentecost establishes one of the most basic gestures of Christian life: joining hands with others across boundaries that divide.

In joining hands, Christians follow the pattern of God's Wisdom made flesh in Jesus, who took on the vulnerability of a creaturely life joined with others in order to heal and save them. The Gospels recount how Jesus stretched out his hand to the leper, but also to Peter when his faith faltered (Matt. 8:3; 14:31). Even Jesus's death did not destroy the redemptive power of this joining. Now, as Peter testifies, God has raised him up and poured out Christ's Spirit, the bond of love, on the community of his followers. The astonished and perplexed crowd in Jerusalem in Acts 2 has two basic questions: "What does this mean?" (v. 12) and "What should we do?" (v. 37). These remain church's questions today. What does it mean that the Spirit promised by Jesus shows up as an uncontrollable wind, driving strangers together? What should we do in order to be a communal embodiment of the Spirit's work of joining? Caught up in the turbulence of the Spirit's work, church is still living into the answers to these questions. Each year, as it celebrates Pentecost, church is reminded of both the gift and the challenge of joining hands.

For a wisdom ecclesiology, Pentecost is not a liturgical afterthought. Starting with Advent, the entire liturgical year traces the story of how God in Christ goes about the work of joining—joining creatures to God and to each other. Christ comes to be God with us by being joined to our flesh. Christ dies and overcomes death so that even that last enemy (1 Cor. 15:26) will not separate us from the perfect communion God intends for us. Church lives out the promise of Christ's life, death, and resurrection by its partial, earthly attempts at communion. The gift of the Spirit at Pentecost is the culmination of God's story of joining, a story that starts with the original grace of creation. This story points ahead of itself to the perfect communion of the end times, and sets the template for what church is to be about in the meantime. Following Pentecost is the longest run of ordinary time in the church year—a Spirit-filled space for church to live into the practice of joining hands.

Both in the original setting of the story and in church life today, the meaning of Pentecost drives the followers of Jesus well beyond their comfort zone. Believers often find it tempting to regard the coming of the Spirit as a reason to erect barriers between themselves and others. Already in the New Testament correspondence, Paul complains that the gifts of the Spirit are being used to exalt some believers over others and divide the community into insiders and outsiders (1 Cor. 12–14). Like the rush of a violent wind, the Spirit at Pentecost blows away these proprietary and divisive spirits and creates instead an unbounded community of mutual gift (Acts 2:44–47). The power of the Spirit is the power of love.[1] Life in the Spirit is life that is opened

---

1. I am here following the pneumatology of contemporary Pentecostal theologians Amos Yong and Frank Macchia. See Frank D. Macchia, *Justified in the Spirit: Creation, Redemp-*

toward the other. The Spirit's promise to us and our children (Acts 2:39) is to form us into a community whose life has a centrifugal force, always being driven toward others in mutual giving and receiving. As Peter insists in his Pentecost sermon, the promise of the Spirit is not just for those near and dear to us: it is "for all who are far away, everyone whom the Lord our God calls to him" (Acts 2:39). In only a few chapters, a shocked and scandalized Peter will discover just how far God's promise of the Spirit travels: beyond the Jewish Diaspora to the unclean world of Gentiles (Acts 11:1–18). Christians are still struggling to establish a communal life that embraces those who are far off, a shared life that is as rich and varied as the human race. Joining hands across barriers that divide us is subversive work. For church, the pouring out of the Spirit at Pentecost means the ongoing work of unlearning the habits and assumptions that isolate and alienate.

"Repent and be baptized" is Peter's answer to those who ask what they should do in response to the pouring out of the Spirit (Acts 2:38). Baptism is the initiation into a common life of those joined by Christ's Spirit, in which each person's flourishing depends on the flourishing of every other. To be baptized is to join hands with others, to become a member of the motley collection of people who are drawn together as the result of God's choosing, not our own. God intends the company of the baptized to be models for all to see what a life of joining hands looks like. To recognize one another's baptisms is to affirm the work of joining that the Spirit has already accomplished. Unity in Christ is the identity toward which the Spirit drives us. Pentecost is a reminder that our attempts to put up lines of demarcation within the body of Christ are ultimately futile and self-deceiving, no matter how much we continue to cling to them. The repentance Peter calls for must continue as Christians seek to unlearn their arrogance and heal their divisions. No one should go away hungry from the Lord's Table.[2] Ecumenical efforts, both official and grassroots, remain essential to a Pentecost church, because joining hands with other Christians is not an optional extra: it is a yielding to the reality of what the Spirit has done.

tion, and the Triune God (Grand Rapids: Eerdmans, 2010); Amos Yong, Spirit of Love: A Trinitarian Theology of Grace (Waco: Baylor University Press, 2012).

2. John Chrysostom (attributed), "The Catechetical Paschal Homily," in The Services for Holy Week and Easter, trans. Leonida Contos, ed. Spencer T. Kezios (San Francisco: Narthex Press, 1994), 420.

For an ordinary-time ecclesiology, joining hands within and across Christian communities of faith has broader creaturely echoes. Joining hands is a sign of both our creaturely strength and our frailty. It is a reaffirmation that we are members of one human family, created by a God who shows no partiality (Acts 10:34). Pentecost is an emphatic repudiation of Christian complicity with racial, socioeconomic, and nationalist enclosures of the Spirit. It condemns all attempts to absolutize human differences rather than to see them as gifts for the flourishing of the whole. The community of the baptized has continually grieved the Holy Spirit in this regard, and has much to repent of. Instead of being a living testimony to the Spirit poured out on all flesh, church has often been a living contradiction.

The bitter truth is that very little of church history reads like Acts 2:44: "all who believed were together and had all things in common." In an Alice Walker short story, ironically entitled "The Welcome Table," the white reverend says to an elderly black woman who comes to Sunday worship, "Auntie, you know this is not your church." Walker's acerbic ecclesiological comment lays bare his racist assumptions: "As if one could choose the wrong one."[3] For the pastor's all-white congregation, "God, mother, country, earth, church" were all linked together in a death-dealing chain of exclusion: that is why they felt they needed "to throw the old colored woman out."[4] It is one of the great sorrows of the Christian faith that church continues to forfeit the new life the Spirit offers because of its patterns of rejection and exclusion. Every year, Pentecost presents an opportunity for repentance, as Christians acknowledge how reluctant they have been to embrace the Spirit's gift of joining hands. Part of the good news of Pentecost is that church's failures are no match for the Spirit's power. In Walker's story, the old woman is welcomed after all, by Jesus himself, who meets her on the road—not inside the sanctuary. Church has no monopoly on the Spirit's presence and power.

A wisdom ecclesiology refuses to absolutize human differences, but it also refuses to deny them altogether. The logic of Pentecost is not a logic of sameness. It is part of our creaturely finitude to find roots in a particular

---

3. Alice Walker, "The Welcome Table," in *In Love and Trouble: Stories of Black Women* (New York: Mariner Books, repr. ed., 2003), 83.

4. Walker, "The Welcome Table," 84.

place, to be connected by proximity, affinity, and kinship to particular circles of people, to enjoy particular kinds of food, music, and dance. It is part of our creaturely finitude to depend on others who have the natural aptitudes and spiritual gifts that we lack (Eph. 4:15–16). The unity of the baptized has sometimes been elaborated in ways that deny our creaturely embeddedness and particularity, and in this way, too, church has grieved the Spirit. The affirmation in Ephesians 2:15 that Christ's reconciliation creates "one new humanity in place of the two" has given rise to the notion that Christians are a third race, a generic form of humanity that transcends and supersedes the creaturely particularity of Jew and Gentile. According to this construal, Christians are those who have completely left behind the earthly ties of land, family, and culture, and now constitute—as church—a paradigm of human personhood toward which all others are to aspire. The notion of Christians as a third race can suggest that non-Christians, still bound to these markers of creaturely particularity, fall short of full personhood. This notion has been especially devastating for relations between an almost wholly Gentile church and Jews. It leaves the Gentile identity of church unmarked and suggests that the promise of the Spirit renders Jewish identity obsolete.[5] A wisdom ecclesiology relativizes but refuses to deny human particularities. Church does not represent a generic paradigm of personhood. In the story of Pentecost, Cretans and Arabs do not stop being Cretans and Arabs when the Holy Spirit comes in power (Acts 2:11). The Spirit joins followers of Jesus together, but does not erase their creaturely particularities or undermine their common humanity with non-Christians.

Mission

The Pentecost vision of church is of "a great multitude that no one could count, from every nation, from all tribes and peoples and languages" (Rev. 7:9). To this end, church is called to stand, like Woman Wisdom, at the

---

5. Willie James Jennings has made a persuasive case for linking the Western Christian refusal to acknowledge its Gentile identity with the development of the social imaginary of whiteness. See *The Christian Imagination: Theology and the Origins of Race* (New Haven, CT: Yale University Press, 2010).

crossroads, in liminal places of connection and interaction (Prov. 8:2). The doors of church are always open to strangers and wayfarers, to all driven by the Spirit to seek a home there. The standing invitation to join hands with the community of the baptized must be continually renewed, which is why mission, including evangelism, is an essential part of church's calling. Church makes no claim to control the Spirit's movement or to delineate the Spirit's territory. Much of the Spirit's work is unknown, even unimaginable, to us. Yet, like Peter, we gratefully claim the good news we have been shown. The grace we have seen poured out in Jesus Christ is not a stingy grace, and in any case it is not ours to bestow or withhold. Church is a community that is called to rejoice in this grace and to invite others to join in a common life of worship and service.

In an account of church in ordinary time, reciprocity and mutuality are at the heart of mission. All mission begins with a recognition of our common humanity, of being fellow creatures loved and sustained by the same God. Mission also begins with the reality of Pentecost, with God's Spirit poured out on all flesh, so that there is no corner of God's world from which the Spirit is absent. Mission is church's acknowledgment of the incompleteness of its own life. It is an effort to catch up with where the Spirit is already at work. The Spirit's bodily curriculum requires joining hands with those who are far off—geographically and otherwise. It is a slow and difficult curriculum, in which we learn by being joined to people we might otherwise prefer not to associate with. As the gospel is spoken in different cultural inflections, the Spirit breathes new life into dormant parts of Scripture and Christian teaching and exorcises toxic assumptions and patterns that stunt our life together. Only in the presence of "every nation under heaven" (Acts 2:5) can church truly repent and claim the meaning of its baptism. Like Pentecost, the movement of mission is circular, not linear. It is not a mandate to be completed once and for all, whose progress can be charted and mapped. It is, instead, an ongoing rhythm of mutual receiving and giving, listening and speaking. Mission revolves around church's recognition that God has gifts to give us that we can only receive from the hands of others.

Joining hands stands in some tension with understandings of Christian mission in which sending has been elevated to a master image. This image remains popular, though it seems more at home in earlier eras of Western mission that divided up the world into Christian and non-Christian territories than it does in today's complex global picture of Christian growth and decline. In this view, church's core identity is being sent in witness to the world, and everything else church does should be a preparation for this sending. The sending paradigm is often linked to the classical language of Trinitarian missions: the Father sending the Son and the Spirit to redeem and sanctify the creaturely world. Sending is thus a divine activity before it is a human one. Christian mission is a participation in God's mission. God is a sending God, and church is a sent people.

Certainly, there is abundant biblical testimony to the importance of sending and being sent. However, from a wisdom perspective, sending is too narrow to serve as the master image for either church or the Trinitarian life. Rowan Williams notes that, regarding God's Trinitarian life, "what sets Christian faith apart most decisively from even its closest religious relatives, is this picture of the divine life involving receiving as well as giving, depending as well as controlling." What Jesus Christ shows us is that "what we understand by 'God' can't just be power and initiative; it also includes receiving and reflecting back in love and gratitude."[6] There is an eternal pattern of dispossession and receptivity in God. The perfection of God's Trinitarian life is both an initiative and a depending. Always imaging God in terms of the power and initiative of sending short-circuits the mutual patterns of the Trinitarian life and tempts church to understand its own mission in linear ways that lack the genuine mutuality of receiving and depending. This mutuality is better signaled by the metaphor of joining hands. For church in ordinary time, sending is best understood as a means to joining hands. It is not an end in itself.

Joining hands is an apt metaphor for mission as church repents of its colonial past. The modern history of the spread of Christianity has been dismayingly coextensive with colonial cultures, often embracing their civilizational and racial hierarchies and sharing their imperialist aspirations. This collusion with colonial agendas has distorted church's witness and betrayed the reality of Pentecost. When we conceive of mission as the geographic extension of Christian territory or the one-way transmission of a Christian

---

6. Rowan Williams, *Tokens of Trust: An Introduction to Christian Belief* (Louisville: Westminster John Knox, 2007), 66, 68.

message, we forfeit the reciprocal dynamic of joining hands. For "mission in the postcolony," the invitation to baptism must be preceded by church's repentance.[7] The way forward is not to repress the shameful memories of past failures of mutuality but to trust the power of the Spirit to enter and heal the awkward spaces where alienation and suspicion linger. Church's ongoing efforts to truly become brothers and sisters in Christ, however modest and faltering, are a living into the Pentecost reality of the Spirit poured out on all flesh. It is no accident that a North American Presbyterian logo for the Confession of Belhar (1986) reflects the confession's themes of unity, justice, and reconciliation in the wake of apartheid with the image of hands of different colors joined together.

"A threefold cord is not quickly broken" (Eccles. 4:12). Qohelet's repeated calls to join hands have not received much attention in theologies of mission, but John Mansford Prior, writing from a Muslim-dominant culture in Indonesia, finds that Ecclesiastes provides a helpful guide to "a modest mission in unpredictable times."[8] Unlike their Western counterparts in once culturally established churches, many of today's Christians are poor and wield little cultural and political influence in their society. In contexts where the dominant religious culture provides a constant countertestimony to Christian witness, Prior finds that the fiery passion of the prophets can drag threatened, minority Christian enclaves into extremist, oppositional stances. He commends Qohelet as a model of quiet resilience, a testimony of presence. The book of Ecclesiastes, he finds, can help Christians "put that necessary distance between involvement and obsession, commitment and its inevitable limitations, and truth and its partial formulations."[9] Christians are not called to deny or forfeit what they know. But what they confess about the power and freedom of the Spirit rightly inspires a gentleness and reverence toward religious others (1 Pet. 3:16). In our unpredictable times, Qohelet is a biblical voice that church needs to pay attention to.

---

7. See Marion Grau, *Rethinking Mission in the Postcolony: Salvation, Society and Subversion* (London: T&T Clark International, 2011).

8. John Mansford Prior, " 'When All the Singing Has Stopped': Ecclesiastes, a Modest Mission in Unpredictable Times," *International Review of Mission* 91 (2002): 7–23.

9. Prior, "'When All the Singing Has Stopped,'" 20.

To the Ends of the Earth

Pentecost is a harvest festival, a celebration of the fruits of God's creation. The images of the Spirit at Pentecost in Acts 2—wind and fire—are elements of the natural world. They belong outdoors. Regardless of where Christian Pentecost celebrations occur, these associations are a reminder that the presence of the Spirit fills the whole world. The Spirit cannot be confined within the precincts of a temple or sanctuary. Christians caught up in the power of the Spirit will find themselves blown far beyond the boundaries of church.

Church's aim is not to establish "the form of life for a whole society."[10] The era of Christendom, that is, of a territorial concept of Christianity, is past. Church has been forced by both external and internal pressures to give up these hegemonic aspirations, which in any case were always to some degree a fiction whose maintenance required trampling on the dignity and freedom of religious others. In a world come of age, the Pentecost vision will not be fulfilled by making the boundaries of church coextensive with the boundaries of human society, so that church may be all in all. As Dietrich Bonhoeffer notes, "The space of the church is not there in order to fight with the world for a piece of its territory," but to proclaim that the whole world is included in God's reconciling purposes.[11] For a wisdom ecclesiology, joining hands is never simply a matter of nurturing bonds among Christians or widening the circle of church, important as those things are. The trajectory of Pentecost is "to the ends of the earth" (Acts 1:8). In its earthly life, church points beyond itself, giving witness to God's love and care for the whole world; and the Spirit of Pentecost drives Christians out into the world to join hands in love and service with all those we meet there, regardless of their religious identity.

Paul exhorts the church in Galatia to "work for the good of all, and especially for those of the family of faith" (Gal. 6:10). This is a reminder to Galatians that the command to love your neighbor as yourself (Gal. 5:14; Lev. 19:18) includes *all* neighbors. The special responsibility to our brothers and sisters in Christ that Paul commends is not a reflection of the boundaries of

10. Cardinal Joseph Ratzinger, *Salt of the Earth: Christianity and the Catholic Church at the End of the Millennium: An Interview with Peter Seewald*, trans. Adrian Walker (San Francisco: Ignatius Press, 1997), 164.

11. Dietrich Bonhoeffer, *Ethics*, Dietrich Bonhoeffer Works, vol. 6 (Minneapolis: Fortress, 2005), 63.

the Spirit's presence or of God's partiality. Paul is not replacing the division between Jew and Gentile with a division between church and world. Victor Paul Furnish notes that Paul's special concern for members of the household of faith "neither rescinds nor compromises the all-inclusive scope of his appeal."[12] Rather, Paul acknowledges the believers' finite location and directs them to begin working for the good of all from there. Joining hands begins within the community of faith, but it does not stop at its borders. Most of the world's problems are far too big for Christians to address on their own. They need help responding to immediate human need and dismantling the social engineering of inequity that defies the reality of the Spirit's coming. Working for the good of all requires joining hands with those who come to these shared tasks with different motivations and ultimate purposes. The power of Pentecost is reflected in initiatives such as the Joining Hands Against Hunger movement, which has creatively brought together very diverse groups to be a major force for combating hunger around the world. Part of church's vocation is to share a vocation with others.

For a wisdom ecclesiology, there is a self-relativizing dimension to church's celebration of Pentecost. Pentecost celebrates the power of the Spirit to join together those who are far off by trespassing human boundaries. This includes the boundaries of church. This was reaffirmed for Dietrich Bonhoeffer as he was drawn deeper into the Abwehr resistance and later shared prison life with other enemies of the Third Reich. As he joined hands with Jews and nonreligious people to subvert the aims of a genocidal regime, Bonhoeffer recognized that here, too, the power of Christ's Spirit was at work. In *Ethics* and *Letters and Papers from Prison*, Christ remains at the center of Bonhoeffer's theology, but he is now glimpsed more and more in places and persons outside church. Charles Marsh describes Bonhoeffer's theological shift: "Those who come to the work of mercy and justice from places outside the church are animated by an energy that the church knows intimately but dares not seek to own."[13] In the vocabulary of Pentecost, church dares not seek to own the Spirit, but it is called to recognize the Spirit's presence ani-

---

12. Victor Paul Furnish, "Uncommon Love and the Common Good: Christians as Citizens in the Letters of Paul," in *In Search of the Common Good*, ed. Dennis P. McCann and Patrick D. Miller (New York: T&T Clark, 2005), 74.

13. Charles Marsh, *Strange Glory: A Life of Dietrich Bonhoeffer* (New York: Alfred A. Knopf, 2014), 314.

mating others and to join hands with them in the work of mercy and justice. Bonhoeffer insists that "the church must participate in the worldly tasks of life in the community—not dominating but helping and serving."[14] Church does not pretend to comprehend the scope of the Spirit's presence, much less to harness it for its own purposes. As trustee of a radically inclusive vision of the communion of all God's creatures, church is called to a life of joining hands that "testifies to the world that it is still the world, namely, the world that is loved and reconciled by God."[15]

14. Dietrich Bonhoeffer, *Letters and Papers from Prison*, Dietrich Bonhoeffer Works, vol. 8 (Minneapolis: Fortress, 2010), 503.

15. Bonhoeffer, *Ethics*, 63.

The Polyphony of Church Life

Lift every voice and sing
Till earth and heaven ring,
Ring with the harmonies of Liberty.

—James Weldon Johnson,
"Lift Every Voice and Sing"

In some of his prison letters, Dietrich Bonhoeffer, who was a lifelong lover and performer of music, explores the theological resonances of polyphony.[1] Polyphony, in a Western musical composition, comprises several independent melody lines that are played or sung together. The harmonies arise from the complex interplay of these different voices. Bonhoeffer sees here an analogy to Christian faith, which "puts us into many different dimensions of life at the same time; in a way we accommodate God and the whole world within us."[2] Sorrow and joy, for example, are both part of "the polyphony

---

1. This versatile theme has been picked up in different ways by Andreas Pangritz, *Polyphonie des Lebens: Zu Dietrich Bonhoeffers "Theologie der Musik"* (Berlin: Alektor Verlag, 1994); John de Gruchy, *Christianity, Art and Transformation: Theological Aesthetics in the Struggle for Justice* (New York: Cambridge University Press, 2001); and Barry Harvey, *Taking Hold of the Real: Dietrich Bonhoeffer and the Profound Worldliness of Christianity* (Eugene, OR: Cascade Books, 2015). I am grateful to Leon Plantinga for helping me write about polyphony.

2. Dietrich Bonhoeffer, *Letters and Papers from Prison*, Dietrich Bonhoeffer Works, vol. 8 (Minneapolis: Fortress, 2010), 405.

of the whole of life," and they often need to be sounded at the same time.[3] Pentecost needs to be celebrated—even amid the sirens of an air-raid shelter. To let our lives get "pushed back into a single dimension" is to miss out on the wholeness of creaturely existence as God intends it. Christian life for Bonhoeffer is intrinsically "multidimensional, polyphonic."[4]

Part 3 of this book can be read as an exploration of the polyphony of church life. As we move through the seasons of the liturgical year, we give voice to the different registers of Christian faith. Living into the story of our faith takes time and requires practice. Yet the point of attending to these voices one by one is that we will learn to hear them sounding all together, in both harmonic consonance and dissonance. The rejoicing of Easter does not disappear as we head into Advent. The suffering of Lent is not silenced by the long stretches of ordinary time. The goal of Christian life lived according to the ongoing rhythms of the liturgical year is polyphony, a harmony of irreducibly distinct voices.

The interplay of voices in polyphonic music typically produces pronounced dissonances. As an ecclesial image, polyphony resists the attempt to impose a grand narrative on church, to pretend that all the dimensions of its life harmonize in aiming at a single, definitive goal. This monophonic totalizing approach remains tempting in ecclesiology, and it usually results in a neglect of church's creatureliness. A wisdom ecclesiology insists that God calls church to live in many different dimensions at once: Christmas and Pentecost, creation and redemption, penultimate realities and ultimate hopes. With this multidimensionality comes complexity and dissonance, a communal life of making new and making do. Welcome to church in ordinary time!

Some polyphonic compositions feature a *cantus firmus*, a steady voice that provides an anchor for the other voices. Bonhoeffer appeals to this image in writing to a newly married Eberhard Bethge, when he says that Bethge's love for his wife is not to be repressed or sublimated into his love for God. Instead, our love for God is the *cantus firmus* to which the contrapuntal themes of all our earthly loves are related, while keeping "their *full independence*."[5] There is no need to try to temper our earthly loves: where the

3. Bonhoeffer, *Letters and Papers from Prison*, 397.
4. Bonhoeffer, *Letters and Papers from Prison*, 405.
5. Bonhoeffer, *Letters and Papers from Prison*, 394 (italics in original).

cantus firmus of our love for God remains clear and strong, "a counterpoint can develop as mightily as it wants." Love for God keeps our other loves from getting out of tune or being cut adrift. "This polyphony," Bonhoeffer tells Bethge, "gives your life wholeness."[6]

For church as well, love for God has to remain the *cantus firmus* as it "lives fully in the midst of life's tasks, questions, successes and failures, experiences, and perplexities."[7] In a world come of age, church is not allowed to retreat into some private religious sphere. It has to love God in the midst of its creaturely loyalties and loves, in what Bonhoeffer calls "the real world." But for both Bonhoeffer and a wisdom ecclesiology, the theological and the concrete hold together: the core reality of the world consists in "its being-loved-by-God."[8] The larger horizon of Bonhoeffer's theology thus requires church to take another step: to anchor our love for God in the *cantus firmus* of God's love for the whole world. All church's efforts at "belonging-together and being-together with other human beings and with the world" are ultimately grounded not just in our love for God, but in God's love for all that is.[9] Church—along with all the rest of God's creatures—is "called to a life that is lived in God's love."[10]

In an account of church in ordinary time, non-Christian humanity and the entirety of nonhuman creation retain their own integrity as creatures loved by God. They are not absorbed into God's purposes for church. God's economy is polyphonic and multidimensional: in the creaturely polyphony anchored by the *cantus firmus* of God's love for the whole world, church is not the only voice sounding in counterpoint. There are other melodies, independent of the one church is singing, that help carry the harmony. Church sings its distinctive song, listening to the other creaturely voices on earth and in heaven, and trusting that the *cantus firmus* of God's love for the whole world will not let it fall out of tune or be cut adrift. Church sings "as mightily as it wants," but its voice is always part of a larger creaturely polyphony.

One of the most spectacular and beloved examples of Western poly-

6. Bonhoeffer, *Letters and Papers from Prison*, 394.

7. Bonhoeffer, *Letters and Papers from Prison*, 486.

8. Dietrich Bonhoeffer, *Ethics*, Dietrich Bonhoeffer Works, vol. 6 (Minneapolis: Fortress, 2005), 233.

9. Bonhoeffer, *Ethics*, 241.

10. Bonhoeffer, *Ethics*, 232.

phonic music is J. S. Bach's *Art of the Fugue*. It comprises fourteen fugues and four canons, which play out increasingly complex contrapuntal developments of a single theme. *Art of the Fugue* is an unfinished work. (Bach died before he could finish the final fugue.) In performance, the final fugue ends abruptly, coming to a sudden stop in the middle of a musical phrase. In the first edition of *Art of the Fugue*, a chorale is appended to the end of it: the chorale's English title is "Before Your Throne I Now Appear." Bonhoeffer finds theological significance here, too, as he contemplates all the lives that have been uprooted and snuffed out prematurely by World War II. Like Bach's *Art of the Fugue*, these lives are fragmented and unfinished. Bonhoeffer recognizes that, as human creatures, we are not in control of our circumstances and thus cannot give our lives the resolution we desire. Instead, he urges the satisfaction of seeing "in this fragment of life that we have, what the whole was intended and designed to be, and of what material it is made." It is enough for our finite lives to be a fragment "in which, even for a short time, the various themes gradually accumulate and harmonize with one another and in which the great counterpoint is sustained from beginning to end." Then at death, Bonhoeffer says, we can sing Bach's final chorale as we approach God's throne of grace, trusting in Christ's mercy.[11]

Bonhoeffer is reflecting on the lives of individual Christians, but there is wisdom here for church as well. Church life never achieves final resolution. It is a creaturely life, always imperfect and unfinished; yet there is glory in the ordinary. It is enough if the various themes of Christian life—creation and redemption, giving and rejoicing, making do and joining hands—gradually accumulate and harmonize with one another. By the power of the Spirit, these distinct, sometimes dissonant, voices do not drop out of church's song but are sustained from beginning to end. In this glimpse of what the whole was intended to be, church gives thanks to God for its earthly life. Anchored by the *cantus firmus* of God's love for the whole world, church—along with Bonhoeffer—does not see fit "to complain about this fragmentary life of ours, but rather even to be glad of it."[12]

11. Bonhoeffer, *Letters and Papers from Prison*, 306.
12. Bonhoeffer, *Letters and Papers from Prison*, 306.

Works Cited

Aletti, Jean-Noël. *Colossiens 1, 15–20*. Analecta Biblica 91. Rome: Biblical Institute Press, 1981.

Aquinas, Thomas. *Summa Theologiae*. In *Basic Writings of Saint Thomas Aquinas*. Edited by Anton C. Pegis. New York: Random House, 1945.

Athanasius. "On the Incarnation of the Word." In *Christology of the Later Fathers*. Edited and translated by E. R. Hardy. Philadelphia: Westminster, 1954.

Augustine. *City of God*. Translated by Gerald G. Walsh, SJ, et al. Introduction by Etienne Gilson. Garden City, NY: Image Books, 1958.

———. *Confessions*. Translated by Maria Boulding. Hyde Park, NY: New City Press, 2001.

———. *De Doctrina Christiana*. Translated by R. P. H. Green. Oxford: Clarendon Press, 1995.

———. *De Trinitate*. In *Corpus Christianorum*, Series Latina, vol. 50. Turnhout, Belgium: Brepols, 1968.

———. *Expositions of the Psalms*. In *Nicene and Post-Nicene Fathers*. First Series. Vol. 8. Reprint, Peabody, MA: Hendrickson Publishers, 1994.

———. *The Literal Meaning of Genesis*. In *The Works of Saint Augustine*. Vol. 1/13: *On Genesis*. Hyde Park, NY: New City Press, 2002.

———. "Sermon 16A." In *The Works of Saint Augustine: A Translation for the 21st Century*. Vol. 3/1: *Sermons 1–19*. Brooklyn, NY: New City Press, 1990.

Balthasar, Hans Urs von. *Mysterium Paschale*. Translated by Aidan Nichols. Grand Rapids: Eerdmans, 1993.

Baptism, Eucharist and Ministry. Faith and Order Paper no. 111. Geneva: World Council of Churches, 1982.

Barth, Karl. *Church Dogmatics*, II/1. Edited by G. W. Bromiley and T. F. Torrance. Edinburgh: T&T Clark, 1957.

———. *Church Dogmatics*, III/2. Translated by Harold Knight, G. W. Bromiley, J. K. S. Reid, and R. H. Fuller. Edinburgh: T&T Clark, 1960.

———. *Church Dogmatics*, IV/1. Edited by G. W. Bromiley and T. F. Torrance. Translated by G. W. Bromiley. New York: T&T Clark, 1956, 2004.

———. *Church Dogmatics*, IV/4: *The Christian Life. Lecture Fragments.* Translated by G. W. Bromiley. Grand Rapids: Eerdmans, 1981.

———. *Dogmatics in Outline*. Translated by G. T. Thomson. New York: Harper and Row, 1959.

———. *Kirchliche Dogmatik*, IV/2. Zürich: Evangelischer Verlag, 1955.

———. "The Real Church." *Scottish Journal of Theology* 3 no. 4 (1950).

Bauckham, Richard. *The Bible and Ecology: Rediscovering the Community of Creation*. Waco, TX: Baylor University Press, 2010.

———. "Where Is Wisdom to Be Found? Colossians 1:15–20 (2)." In *Reading Texts, Seeking Wisdom*, edited by D. F. Ford and G. Stanton. London: SCM Press, 2003.

Bavinck, Herman. *The Doctrine of God*. Grand Rapids: Eerdmans, 1951.

Berry, Thomas. *The Christian Future and the Fate of Earth*. Maryknoll, NY: Orbis, 2009.

Berry, Wendell. *Home Economics*. New York: North Point, 1987.

———. *Jayber Crow: A Novel*. Washington, DC: Counterpoint, 2000.

———. "Manifesto: The Mad Farmer Liberation Front." In *The Selected Poems of Wendell Berry*. Berkeley, CA: Counterpoint, 1998.

Beste, Jennifer. *God and the Victim: Traumatic Intrusions on Grace and Freedom*. New York: Oxford University Press, 2007.

Bethge, Eberhard. *Dietrich Bonhoeffer: A Biography*. Revised edition. Minneapolis: Fortress, 2000.

Billings, J. Todd. *Calvin, Participation, and the Gift*. Oxford: Oxford University Press, 2007.

———. "John Milbank's Theology of the 'Gift' and Calvin's Theology of Grace: A Critical Comparison." *Modern Theology* 21, no. 1 (January 2005).

Boesak, Allan. *Black and Reformed: Apartheid, Liberation and the Calvinist Tradition*. Maryknoll, NY: Orbis, 1984.

Boff, Leonardo. *Passion of Christ, Passion of the World*. Maryknoll, NY: Orbis, 2001.

Bonhoeffer, Dietrich. *Berlin: 1932–1933*. Dietrich Bonhoeffer Works, vol. 12. Minneapolis: Fortress, 2009.

———. *Conspiracy and Imprisonment, 1940–1945*. Dietrich Bonhoeffer Works, vol. 16. Minneapolis: Fortress, 2006.

———. *Ethics*. Dietrich Bonhoeffer Works, vol. 6. Minneapolis: Fortress, 2005.

———. *Letters and Papers from Prison*. Dietrich Bonhoeffer Works, vol. 8. Minneapolis: Fortress, 2010.

———. *Life Together*. Dietrich Bonhoeffer Works, vol. 5. Minneapolis: Fortress, 1996.

———. *Sanctorum Communio: A Theological Study of the Sociology of the Church*. Dietrich Bonhoeffer Works, vol. 1. Minneapolis: Fortress, 2009.

———. *A Testament to Freedom: The Essential Writings of Dietrich Bonhoeffer*. Edited by Geffrey B. Kelly and F. Burton Nelson. San Francisco: HarperCollins, 1990.

———. *Theological Education at Finkenwalde: 1935–1937*. Dietrich Bonhoeffer Works, vol. 14. Minneapolis: Fortress, 2013.

———. *Theological Education Underground: 1937–1940*. Dietrich Bonhoeffer Works, vol. 15. Minneapolis: Fortress, 2012.

Book of Confessions. Part 1 of *The Constitution of the Presbyterian Church (USA)*. Louisville: The Office of the General Assembly, Presbyterian Church (USA), 2016.

Bourdieu, Pierre. *Outline of a Theory of Practice*. Translated by Richard Nice. Cambridge, UK: Cambridge University Press, 1977.

Bright, John. *The Authority of the Old Testament*. Nashville: Abingdon, 1967.

Brock, Rita Nakashima, Claudia Camp, and Serene Jones, eds. *Setting the Table: Women in Theological Conversation*. St. Louis: Chalice Press, 1995.

Brown, Raymond E. *The Gospel according to John*. Vol. 1. New York: Doubleday, 1966.

Brown, William P. *The Seven Pillars of Creation: The Bible, Science, and the Ecology of Wonder*. Oxford: Oxford University Press, 2010.

Brunner, Emil. *Revelation and Reason*. Philadelphia: Westminster, 1946.

Burrell, David B. "Creation as Original Grace." In *God, Grace, and Creation*, vol. 55 of *The Annual Publication of the College Theology Society*, edited by Philip J. Rossi. Maryknoll, NY: Orbis, 2010.

Busch, Eberhard. "Reformed Strength in Its Denominational Weakness." In *Re-*

formed Theology: Identity and Ecumenicity, edited by Wallace Alston and Michael Welker. Grand Rapids: Eerdmans, 2003.

Calvin, John. *Commentary on the Book of the Prophet Isaiah*, vol. 4. Translated by William Pringle. Edinburgh: Calvin Translation Society, 1853.

———. "The Epistle of Paul to the Ephesians." In *Calvin's New Testament Commentaries*, vol. 11. Edited by David W. Torrance and Thomas F. Torrance. Translated by T. H. L. Parker. Grand Rapids: Eerdmans, 1965.

———. *Institutes of the Christian Religion*. Edited by John T. McNeill. Translated by Ford Lewis Battles. Philadelphia: Westminster, 1960.

Cardman, Francine. "Myth, History, and the Beginnings of the Church." In *Governance, Accountability, and the Future of the Catholic Church*, edited by Francis Oakley and Bruce Russett. New York: Continuum, 2004.

Carter, J. Kameron. "An Unlikely Convergence: W. E. B. Du Bois, Karl Barth, and the Problem of the Imperial God-Man." *CR: The New Centennial Review* 11 (2011): 167–224.

Chardin, P. Teilhard de. *The Future of Man*. New York: Image Books, 2004.

Collins, Francis S. *The Language of God: A Scientist Presents Evidence for Belief*. New York: Free Press, 2006.

Connerton, Paul. *How Societies Remember*. Cambridge, UK: Cambridge University Press, 1989.

Conradie, Ernst M. *An Ecological Christian Anthropology: At Home on Earth?* Burlington, VT: Ashgate, 2005.

Copeland, Shawn. *Enfleshing Freedom: Body, Race, and Being*. Minneapolis: Fortress, 2009.

Cosmos: A Spacetime Odyssey. National Geographic Television Productions, 2014.

Craigo-Snell, Shannon. *The Empty Church: Theater, Theology, and Bodily Hope*. Oxford: Oxford University Press, 2014.

Davis, Ellen F. *Proverbs, Ecclesiastes, and the Song of Songs*. Westminster Bible Companion. Louisville: Westminster John Knox, 2000.

Depperman, Klaus. *Melchior Hoffman*. Translated by Malcolm Wren. London: T&T Clark, 1987.

Doyle, Dennis M., Timothy J. Furry, and Pascal D. Bazzell, eds. *Ecclesiology and Exclusion: Boundaries of Being and Belonging in Postmodern Times*. Maryknoll, NY: Orbis, 2012.

Dulles, Avery. *A Church to Believe In*. New York: Crossroad, 1985.

─────. *Models of the Church*. New York: Doubleday, 1974.

Dykstra, Craig, and Dorothy C. Bass. "Times of Yearning, Practices of Faith." In *Practicing Our Faith*, edited by Dorothy C. Bass. 2nd edition. San Francisco: John Wiley and Sons, 2010.

Edwards, Jonathan. *Ethical Writings*. The Works of Jonathan Edwards, vol. 8. Edited by Paul Ramsey. New Haven: Yale University Press, 1989.

─────. *The "Miscellanies," a–500*. The Works of Jonathan Edwards, vol. 13. Edited by Thomas A. Schafer. New Haven: Yale University Press, 1994.

─────. *Religious Affections*. The Works of Jonathan Edwards, vol. 2. Edited by John E. Smith. New Haven: Yale University Press, 1959.

Eliot, T. S. "Ash Wednesday." In *Collected Poems 1909–1962*. Orlando, FL: Harcourt, Brace, 1963.

Farley, Margaret A. "No One Goes Away Hungry from the Table of the Lord." In *Practice What You Preach: Virtues, Ethics, and Power in the Lives of Pastoral Ministers and Their Congregations,* edited by James F. Keenan and Joseph Kotva Jr. Franklin, WI: Sheed and Ward, 1999.

Ferguson, Ron. *George MacLeod: Founder of the Iona Community*. Glasgow: Wild Goose Publications, 2001.

Fontaine, Carole R. *Smooth Words: Women, Proverbs and Performance in Biblical Wisdom*. Journal for the Study of the Old Testament Supplement Series, vol. 356. Sheffield, UK: Sheffield Academic Press, 2002.

Ford, David. "Jesus Christ, the Wisdom of God." In *Reading Texts, Seeking Wisdom: Scripture and Theology*, edited by David F. Ford and Graham Stanton. Grand Rapids: Eerdmans, 2004.

Francis. *Laudato si'*. Encyclical Letter on Care for Our Common Home. Vatican Website. May 24, 2015. http://w2.vatican.va/content/francesco/en/encyclicals/documents/papa-francesco_20150524_enciclica-laudato-si.html.

Fretheim, Terence E. *Creation Untamed: The Bible, God, and Natural Disasters*. Grand Rapids: Baker Academic, 2010.

─────. *God and World in the Old Testament: A Relational Theology of Creation*. Nashville: Abingdon, 2005.

Fulkerson, Mary McClintock. *Places of Redemption: Theology for a Worldly Church*. Oxford: Oxford University Press, 2007.

Fulkerson, Mary McClintock, and Marcia W. Mount Shoop. *A Body Broken, a Body Betrayed: Race, Memory, and Eucharist in White-Dominant Churches*. Eugene, OR: Cascade Books, 2015.

Gandolfo, Elizabeth. "A Truly Human Incarnation: Recovering a Place for Nativity in Contemporary Christology." *Theology Today* 70, no. 4 (2013).

Garrigan, Siobhán. *Beyond Ritual: Sacramental Theology after Habermas.* Hampshire, UK: Ashgate, 2004.

———. *The Real Peace Process: Worship, Politics and the End of Sectarianism.* London: Equinox, 2010.

George, Kondothra M. "Editorial." *The Ecumenical Review* 44 (January 1992).

Gorringe, Timothy. *Redeeming Time: Education through Atonement.* London: Darton, Longman and Todd, 1986.

———. *A Theology of the Built Environment: Justice, Empowerment, Redemption.* Cambridge, UK: Cambridge University Press, 2002.

Gregersen, Niels. "The Cross of Christ in an Evolutionary World." *Dialog: A Journal of Theology* 40 (2001).

Gregory of Nazianzus. *Theological Orations* 30.6. In *Nicene and Post-Nicene Fathers*, second series, vol. 7, edited by Philip Schaff. Peabody, MA: Hendrickson Publishers.

———. "To Cledonius the Priest against Apollinarius (Letter 101)." In *Nicene and Post-Nicene Fathers*, second series, vol. 7, edited by Philip Schaff. Peabody, MA: Hendrickson Publishers.

Gregory of Nyssa. *Address on Religious Instruction* 24. Translated by Cyril C. Richardson. In *Christology of the Later Fathers*, edited by E. R. Hardy. Philadelphia: Westminster, 1954.

Grenz, Stanley. *The Social God and the Relational Self: A Trinitarian Theology of the Imago Dei.* Louisville: Westminster John Knox, 2001.

Gustafson, James. *Treasure in Earthen Vessels: The Church as a Human Community.* 3rd edition. Louisville: Westminster John Knox, 2009.

Hardy, Daniel W., and David F. Ford. *Jubilate: Theology in Praise.* London: Darton, Longman and Todd, 1984.

Hauerwas, Stanley. *The Peaceable Kingdom: A Primer in Christian Ethics.* Notre Dame, IN: University of Notre Dame Press, 1983.

Haught, John. *God after Darwin.* Boulder, CO: Westview Press, 2008.

Herbert, George. *The Country Parson, The Temple.* The Classics of Western Spirituality. Edited by John N. Wall Jr. New York: Paulist Press, 1981.

Hoeksema, Herman. *Reformed Dogmatics.* Grand Rapids: Reformed Free Publishing Association, 1966.

Irenaeus. *Against Heresies.* In *The Ante-Nicene Fathers*, vol. 1, edited by Alexander Roberts and James Donaldson. New York: Charles Scribner's Sons, 1903.

Jennings, Willie James. *Acts.* Belief: A Theological Commentary on the Bible. Louisville: Westminster John Knox, 2017.

———. "The Aesthetic Struggle and Ecclesial Vision." In *Black Practical Theology*, edited by Dale P. Andrews and Robert London Smith Jr. Waco, TX: Baylor University Press, 2015.

———. *The Christian Imagination.* New Haven: Yale University Press, 2010.

Jenson, Robert W. "The Church's Responsibility for the World." In *The Two Cities of God: The Church's Responsibility for the Earthly City*, edited by Carl E. Braaten and Robert W. Jenson. Grand Rapids: Eerdmans, 1997.

Johnson, Mark. *The Meaning of the Body: Aesthetics of Human Understanding.* Chicago: University of Chicago Press, 2007.

Jones, Joe R. *A Grammar of Christian Faith: Systematic Explorations in Christian Life and Doctrine.* Vol. 1. Lanham, MD: Rowman and Littlefield, 2002.

Jones, Serene. *Trauma and Grace: Theology in a Ruptured World.* Louisville: Westminster John Knox, 2009.

Julian of Norwich. *The Showings of Julian of Norwich.* Edited by Denise N. Baker. New York: W. W. Norton, 2005.

Keller, Catherine. *On the Mystery: Discerning Divinity in Process.* Minneapolis: Fortress, 2008.

Kelsey, David H. *Eccentric Existence: A Theological Anthropology.* 2 vols. Louisville: Westminster John Knox, 2009.

———. *The Uses of Scripture in Recent Theology.* Minneapolis: Fortress, 1975.

Keshgegian, Flora. *Redeeming Memories: A Theology of Healing and Transformation.* Nashville: Abingdon, 2000.

King, Martin Luther, Jr. "Letter from a Birmingham Jail." In *A Testament of Hope: The Essential Writings and Speeches of Martin Luther King, Jr.*, edited by James M. Washington. San Francisco: HarperSanFrancisco, 1991.

Küng, Hans. *The Church.* Translated by Ray Ockenden and Rosaleen Ockenden. London: Burns and Oates, 1967.

Lash, Nicholas. *Theology for Pilgrims.* London: Darton, Longman and Todd, 2008.

Lathrop, Gordon W. *Holy Ground: A Liturgical Cosmology.* Minneapolis: Fortress, 2003.

Lear, Jonathan. *Radical Hope: Ethics in the Face of Cultural Devastation.* Cambridge, MA: Harvard University Press, 2008.

"Letter to Diognetus." In *Early Christian Fathers.* Edited and translated by Cyril C. Richardson. New York: Macmillan, 1970.

Lindbeck, George A. *The Church in a Postliberal Age.* Edited by James J. Buckley. Grand Rapids: Eerdmans, 2002.

Locher, Gottfried W. *Zwingli's Thought: New Perspectives.* Leiden: Brill, 1981.

Macchia, Frank D. *Justified in the Spirit: Creation, Redemption, and the Triune God.* Grand Rapids: Eerdmans, 2010.

MacKinnon, D. M. "The Evangelical Imagination." In *Philosophy and the Burden of Theological Honesty: A Donald MacKinnon Reader*, edited by John C. McDowell. New York: T&T Clark, 2011.

———. *The Stripping of the Altars.* London: Collins, Fontana Library, 1969.

Madsen, Richard P. "Catholicism as Chinese Folk Religion." In *China and Christianity: Burdened Past, Hopeful Future*, edited by Stephen Uhalley Jr. and Xiaoxin Wu. Armonk, NY: M. E. Sharpe, 2001.

McDougall, Dorothy C. *The Cosmos as the Primary Sacrament.* New York: Peter Lang, 2003.

McFague, Sallie. *The Body of God: An Ecological Theology.* Minneapolis: Fortress, 1993.

Mead, Sidney E. *The Lively Experiment: The Shaping of Christianity in America.* New York: Harper and Row, 1963.

Meeks, Wayne. "The 'Haustafeln' and American Slavery: A Hermeneutical Challenge." In *Theology and Ethics in Paul and His Interpreters*, edited by Eugene H. Lovering Jr. and Jerry L. Sumney. Nashville: Abingdon, 1996.

———. "A Hermeneutics of Social Embodiment." *Harvard Theological Review* 79 (1986): 184.

———. "The Irony of Grace." In *Shaping a Theological Mind: Theological Context and Methodology*, edited by Darren C. Marks. Burlington, VT: Ashgate, 2002.

Merleau-Ponty, Maurice. *Phenomenology of Perception.* New York: Routledge, 1962.

———. "Philosopher and His Shadow." In *Signs.* Translated by Richard C. McCleary. Evanston, IL: Northwestern University Press, 1964.

Merton, Thomas. *The Seven-Storey Mountain.* New York: Harcourt, Brace, 1948.

Miles, Margaret R. *Bodies in Society: Essays on Christianity in Contemporary Culture*. Eugene, OR: Cascade, 2008.

Miller, Vassar. "Brute Fact." In *If I Had Wheels or Love: Collected Poems of Vassar Miller*. Dallas: Southern Methodist University Press, 1991.

Moltmann, Jürgen. *The Church in the Power of the Spirit*. Translated by Margaret Kohl. New York: Harper and Row, 1977.

———. *The Coming of God: Christian Eschatology*. Translated by Margaret Kohl. Minneapolis: Fortress, 1996.

Muers, Rachel. "The Holy Spirit, the Voice of Nature and Environmental Prophecy." *Scottish Journal of Theology* 67, no. 3 (2014): 323–39.

Murphy, Roland E. "Wisdom and Creation." In *Wisdom and Psalms*. Edited by Athalya Brenner and Carole Fontaine. Sheffield, UK: Sheffield Academic Press, 1998.

Neuner, J., and J. Dupuis, eds. *The Christian Faith in the Doctrinal Documents of the Catholic Church*. New York: Alba House, 1982.

Niebuhr, H. Richard. *Christ and Culture*. New York: Harper and Row, 1975.

Nussbaum, Martha C. *Upheavals of Thought: The Intelligence of Emotions*. Cambridge, UK: Cambridge University Press, 2003.

Pauw, Amy Plantinga. "Christ, the Receiver of Gifts." In *The Gift of Theology: The Contribution of Kathryn Tanner*, edited by Rosemary P. Carbine and Hilda P. Koster. Minneapolis: Fortress, 2015.

———. "The Holy Spirit and Scripture." In *The Lord and Giver of Life: Perspectives on Constructive Pneumatology*, edited by David H. Jensen. Louisville: Westminster John Knox, 2008.

———. "The Lay Practice of Scripture." In *Sharper Than a Two-Edged Sword: Preaching, Teaching, and Living the* Bible, edited by Michael Root and James J. Buckley. Grand Rapids: Eerdmans, 2008.

———. *Proverbs and Ecclesiastes*. Belief: A Theological Commentary on the Bible. Louisville: Westminster John Knox, 2015.

———. *The Supreme Harmony of All: The Trinitarian Theology of Jonathan Edwards*. Grand Rapids: Eerdmans, 2002.

Plested, Marcus. "Wisdom in the Fathers: An (Eastern) Orthodox Perspective." In *Encounter between Eastern Orthodoxy and Radical Orthodoxy: Transfiguring the World through the Word*, edited by Adrian Pabst and Christoph Schneider. Farnham, UK: Ashgate, 2009.

Prior, John Mansford. "'When All the Singing Has Stopped': Ecclesiastes, a

Modest Mission in Unpredictable Times." *International Review of Mission* 91 (2002).

Pritchard, James B., ed. *The Ancient Near East: An Anthology of Texts and Pictures.* Princeton: Princeton University Press, 1958.

Rambo, Shelly. *Spirit and Trauma: A Theology of Remaining.* Louisville: Westminster John Knox, 2010.

Rasmussen, Larry. "Sightings of Primal Visions: Community and Ecology." In *Character and Scripture: Moral Formation, Community, and Biblical Interpretation,* edited by William P. Brown. Grand Rapids: Eerdmans, 2002.

Ratzinger, Cardinal Joseph. *Salt of the Earth: Christianity and the Catholic Church at the End of the Millennium: An Interview with Peter Seewald.* Translated by Adrian Walker. San Francisco: Ignatius Press, 1997.

Rivera, Mayra. *Poetics of the Flesh.* Durham, NC: Duke University Press, 2015.

Roberts, J. Deotis. *Liberation and Reconciliation: A Black Theology.* Philadelphia: Westminster, 1971.

Robinson, Marilynne. *Lila: A Novel.* New York: Farrar, Straus and Giroux, 2014.

Rogers, Eugene F. *After the Spirit: A Constructive Pneumatology from Sources outside the Modern West.* Grand Rapids: Eerdmans, 2005.

Rossi, Philip J. "Creation as Grace of Radical Dependence." In *God, Grace, and Creation.* Annual Publication of the College Theology Society, vol. 55, edited by Philip J. Rossi. Maryknoll, NY: Orbis, 2010.

Russell, Letty. *Human Liberation in a Feminist Perspective.* Philadelphia: Westminster, 1974.

Schleiermacher, Friedrich. *On Religion: Speeches to Its Cultured Despisers.* Translated by John Oman. Louisville: Westminster John Knox, 1994.

Schmitz, Kenneth L. *The Gift: Creation.* Milwaukee: Marquette University Press, 1982.

Silverstein, Shel. *The Giving Tree.* New York: Harper and Row, 1964.

Simons, Menno. "Brief Confession on the Incarnation (1544)." In *The Complete Works of Menno Simons.* Edited by J. C. Wenger. Harrisonburg, VA: Herald Press, 1956.

Smith, Maf, John Whitelegg, and Nick Williams. *Greening the Built Environment.* London: Earthscan Publications, 1998.

Smith, Ted A. *The New Measures: A Theological History of Democratic Practice.* Cambridge, UK: Cambridge University Press, 2007.

————. "Redeeming Critique: Resignations to the Cultural Turn in Christian Ethics." *Journal of the Society of Christian Ethics* 24, no. 2 (Fall 2004).

————. "Theories of Practice." In *The Wiley Blackwell Companion to Practical Theology*, edited by Bonnie J. Miller-McLemore. Oxford: Blackwell, 2012.

Sokolowski, Robert. "Creation and Christian Understanding." In *God and Creation: An Ecumenical Symposium*, edited by David Burrell and Bernard McGinn. Notre Dame, IN: University of Notre Dame Press, 1990.

Sonderegger, Katherine. *Systematic Theology.* Vol. 1. Minneapolis: Fortress, 2015.

Soskice, Janet Martin. "Creation and Participation." *Theology Today* 68, no. 3 (2011).

————. "The Ends of Man and the Future of God." In *The End of the World and the Ends of God: Science and Theology on Eschatology*, edited by John Polkinghorne and Michael Welker. Harrisburg, PA: Trinity Press International, 2000.

Stubbs, David L. "Practices, Core Practices, and the Work of the Holy Spirit." *Journal for Christian Theological Research* 9 (2004).

Tanner, Kathryn. *Economy of Grace.* Minneapolis: Fortress, 2005.

————. *God and Creation in Christian Theology: Tyranny or Empowerment?* Oxford: Blackwell, 1988.

————. *Jesus, Humanity and the Trinity.* Minneapolis: Fortress, 2001.

————. *Theories of Culture.* Minneapolis: Fortress, 1997.

Taylor, Charles. *The Ethics of Authenticity.* Cambridge: Harvard University Press, 1991.

Tertullian. *On the Flesh of Christ.* Translated by Ernest Evans. London: SPCK, 1956.

————. *Treatise on the Resurrection.* Translated by Ernest Evans. London: SPCK, 1960.

Thalassios the Libyan. *The Philokalia.* Vol. 2. London: Faber and Faber, 1981.

Thurman, Howard. *Jesus and the Disinherited.* Boston: Beacon Press, 1976.

————. "What Shall I Do with My Life?" In *Callings: Twenty Centuries of Christian Wisdom on Vocation*, edited by William C. Placher. Grand Rapids: Eerdmans, 2005.

Tinker, George E. *Spirit and Resistance: Political Theology and American Indian Liberation.* Minneapolis: Fortress, 2004.

Tjørham, Ola. *Visible Church—Visible Unity.* Collegeville, MN: Liturgical Press, 2004.

Townes, Emilie M. "'The Doctor Ain't Taking No Sticks': Race and Medicine in the African American Community." In *Embracing the Spirit: Womanist Perspectives on Hope, Salvation, and Transformation*, edited by Emilie M. Townes. Maryknoll, NY: Orbis, 1997.

Van Til, Cornelius. *Common Grace and the Gospel,* Reprint edition. Phillipsburg, NJ: Protestant and Reformed, 1995.

Van Dyk, Leanne. "The Gifts of God for the People of God: Christian Feminism and Sacramental Theology." In *Feminist and Womanist Essays in Reformed Dogmatics*, edited by Amy Plantinga Pauw and Serene Jones. Louisville: Westminster John Knox, 2006.

Vatican II. *Gaudium et Spes.*

Verhey, Allen, and Joseph S. Harvard. *Ephesians.* Belief: A Theological Commentary on the Bible. Louisville: Westminster John Knox, 2011.

Walker, Alice. "The Welcome Table." In *In Love and Trouble: Stories of Black Women.* New York: Mariner Books, repr. ed., 2003.

Walker, Andrew. "Thoroughly Modern: Sociological Reflections on the Charismatic Movement from the End of the Twentieth Century." In *Charismatic Christianity: Sociological Perspectives*, edited by Stephen Hunt, Malcolm Hamilton, and Tony Walter. New York: Palgrave Macmillan, 1997.

Walls, Andrew. "Christianity in the Non-Western World: A Study in the Serial Nature of Christian Expansion." *Studies in World Christianity* 1, no. 1 (1995).

Webster, John. "The Church and the Perfection of God." In *The Community of the Word: Toward an Evangelical Ecclesiology*, edited by Mark Husbands and Daniel J. Treier. Downers Grove, IL: IVP Academic, 2005.

———. "*Non ex aequo*: God's Relation to Creatures." In *God without Measure: Working Papers in Christian Theology.* Vol. 1: *God and the Works of God.* London: Bloomsbury, 2016.

———. "*Omnia . . . Pertractantur in Sacra Doctrina Sub Ratione Dei.* On the Matter of Christian Theology." In *God without Measure: Working Papers in Christian Theology.* Vol. 1: *God and the Works of God.* London: Bloomsbury, 2016.

Weil, Simone. *Waiting for God.* New York: Harper and Row, 1973.

Williams, Rowan. "Augustine and the Psalms." *Interpretation* 58, no. 1 (January 2004).

————. *Faith in the Public Square.* London: Bloomsbury, 2012.

————. *On Christian Theology.* Oxford: Blackwell, 2000.

————. *A Ray of Darkness: Sermons and Reflections.* Cambridge, MA: Cowley, 1995.

————. *Tokens of Trust: An Invitation to Christian Belief.* Louisville: Westminster John Knox, 2007.

Willis, David. *Notes on the Holiness of God.* Grand Rapids: Eerdmans, 2002.

Wink, Walter. *Engaging the Powers: Discernment and Resistance in a World of Domination.* Minneapolis: Fortress, 1992.

————. *Unmasking the Powers.* Philadelphia: Fortress, 1986.

Winner, Lauren F. *Still: Notes on a Mid-Faith Crisis.* New York: HarperOne, 2013.

Witherington, Ben, III. *Jesus the Sage: The Pilgrimage of Wisdom.* Minneapolis: Fortress, 1994.

Yong, Amos. *Spirit of Love: A Trinitarian Theology of Grace.* Waco: Baylor University Press, 2012.

Zizioulas, John D. *Being as Communion: Studies in Personhood and the Church.* Crestwood, NY: St. Vladimir's Seminary Press, 1985.

————. "Priest of Creation." In *Environmental Stewardship: Critical Perspectives—Past and Present*, edited by R. J. Berry. London: T&T Clark, 2006.

Index of Authors

Index of Authors

INDEX OF AUTHORS

Index of Subjects

Index of Scripture References

Index of Scripture References

Mark

6:5	77
13:22	78n21
15:40	74–75

Luke

1:37	126
1:51–53	133
2:30	127
2:34–35	76
2:52	75
7:11–15	77
8:2–3	75
13:10–13	81
24	119
24:27	119
24:31	97
24:35	119
24:36	79

John

1:1–18	56, 57
1:3	55
1:5	57
1:14	110
3:6	70
3:8	105
3:16	28, 43
4:48	78
20:26	79

Acts

1:8	158
2	150, 151, 158
2:2	150
2:5	155
2:11	154
2:12	151
2:16–18	150
2:22	77
2:37	151
2:38	152
2:39	152
2:44	153
2:44–47	151
3:21	83
10:34	153
11:1–18	152
17:28	126

Romans

4:17	144
8:17	121
8:21	122
8:21–22	109
8:23	53–54, 112
8:25–26	121
8:26	114
8:35–39	79
8:38–39	50
9:4	125
10:14–17	96
10:17	15, 63
12:8	114

1 Corinthians

1:23–24	69
1:24–25	15–16
4:8	80
8	118
10:16	95
10:16–17	93
11	101
11:22	101
11:26	103
11:27	101
11:29	101
11:31	101
12–14	151
12:21	4, 101
15:26	151
15:28	109, 125
15:42	149

2 Corinthians

3:18	78

4:7 82, 100, 116

4:7	82, 100, 116
4:10	108, 134
5:17	101, 115
8:3	132
8:14	131
8:15	131
12:7	138
12:9	138

Galatians

5:14	158
5:17	110
6:10	158

Ephesians

1:22b–23	83, 102
2:12	99
2:14	82
2:15	154
4:1	123
4:5	98
4:13	37, 125
4:14	124n9
4:15–16	154
5:23	55, 80
5:27	8

Philippians

2:6–7	70
3:20	49, 86
4:4	146

Colossians

1:15	66
1:15–20	56, 57, 59, 68
1:16	62, 64, 89
1:17	55
1:17–18	59
1:18	66
1:20	55, 62, 66
3:18–4:1	65
3:30	81